How to Publish Your Book

Self-Publishing For Authors Made Easy

Shane Millar

TAGLINE PUBLISHING

Tagline Publishing

Also By Shane Millar

Write Better Fiction

The Write Better Fiction Key Beats #0.5

How to Write Brilliant Beginnings #1

How to Plot Your Novel #2

How to Write Novels Fast #3

How to Edit Your Novel #4

How to Publish Your Book #5

More *Write Better Fiction* coming soon...

How to Publish Your Book: Self-Publishing for Authors Made Easy (Write Better Fiction, Book 5)

Published by Tagline Publishing

https://writebetterfiction.com

ISBN (eBook): 978-1-915192-29-5

ISBN (Paperback): 978-1-915192-30-1

Cover designed using Canva

Formatted using Atticus

CONTENTS

To The Alliance of Independent Authors. Thank you for being a valuable source of inspiration, knowledge, and resources.

"At the heart of everything is the mantra, 'Have integrity, add value'. My best advice is to forget about the money and concentrate on making the best possible product you can. If you get it right, the money will follow."

—Joseph Alexander, Self-Published Millionaire

INTRODUCTION

WHAT IS SELF-PUBLISHING?

THE TERM "**SELF-PUBLISHING**" IS misleading.

It conjures up images of starving writers, all alone in their drafty, dank, cold garrets, necking whiskey from battered hip flasks, doing everything by themselves.

Now, there's a depressing thought.

Self-Publishing—despite the work of some fantastic **Independent Authors** and indie-supportive organisations—still gets a bad rap in some circles. This is because people often misunderstand what being an **Independent Author** means.

Self-Publishing (or **Independent Publishing**, which is the term I prefer) is a team sport. When you **Independently Publish**, you'll work with a bunch of people to get your precious little book baby out into the big, wide world, including one or all of the following:

- Cover designers
- Beta readers
- Professional Editors
- Proofreaders
- Other authors

When you **Independently Publish**, writing becomes a creative business (and yes, before you roll your eyes in disdain, creativity and business can co-exist). **Independent Authors** want to produce quality books that delight readers. We don't want to produce sub-par work that only results in a slew of one-star reviews, negative comments, and zero sales.

But, wait!

I know what you're thinking...

Who in the Name of the Literary Gods is this Guy...

And Why the Hell Should I Listen to Him?

Exit the mind palace and take off the deerstalker there, Sherlock. Who in the name of the literary gods are you... and why the hell should I listen?

Damn, you're good at asking questions!

It's a valid one, though.

I'm Shane, and in 2019, I stopped thinking, talking, and internally obsessing about becoming an author and actually did it. In 2022, I independently published the first four novels in my *Myth & Magic* urban fantasy thriller series under the pen name S. W. Millar, and a series of *Write Better Fiction* craft guides for writers. As well as being an author, I'm a *Fictionary Certified StoryCoach*, developmental editor, podcaster, and an unapologetically nerdy writing craft junkie.

And I'll say this...

It took me way, way too long to hit that publish button.

Hang on. Three years isn't that long, and you just said you've published a ton of books.

True.

And if that were the entire story, I'd agree with you.

Let me take you back to 2010, my writerly friend.

Twelve years ago, I wrote a truly terrible vampire novel (which I'm currently re-writing in the hope I can rescue it from eternal damnation and hellfire), then I did what 99.9% of writers do. I stuck it in a drawer, let it gather dust, and fell into a "sensible" corporate job.

In late 2018, I found that book, skimmed it, and was riddled with self-doubt and imposter syndrome. Who wrote this steaming pile of garbage?

It was bad.

Awful, in fact.

The opening pages were dull, the plot was non-existent, and all the characters sounded the same and lacked depth.

Basically, it wasn't fit to line a rabbit hutch with, never mind being fit for public consumption.

But...

I still wanted to be an author.

That meant writing a book I'd feel comfortable selling, and comfortable letting other people read. It also meant I had to decide how I was going to get my work into the world.

Did I want to pursue **Traditional Publishing**, or **Independently Publish**?

Let's be honest, I didn't know where to start.

So, over the next two years, I did what any self-respecting nerd would do.

I studied.

A lot.

I consumed every book on publishing and the author business I could get my hands on, bought all the courses, and was lucky enough to meet some fantastic author mentors who have been extremely generous with their time and expertise. For the latter, I will be eternally grateful... but...

It was a mission and a half, and life is too short.

I'm writing this because it's the book I wish I had when I first started out in this business. I want to give something back to the author community, and help you self-publish your book.

How to Use This Book

What This Book Is (and What it Isn't)

In this book, you'll learn how to implement **The Thirteen Pillars of Self-Publishing Success**. As the book's title suggests, you'll discover a simple process for **Independently Publishing** books that will satisfy readers.

If you're new to **Independent Publishing**, I suggest you read this handy guide from cover to cover, leveraging each **Pillar** as you go. If you're more experienced, you can visit certain sections if you need a refresher.

There are no rules about how to read books.

This is your author journey and you have to do what's best for you.

How to Publish Your Book: The Structure

Here's a quick overview of what you can expect:

Part 1: Pre-Publishing Prep

Self-Publishing Pillar #1—Pick Your Publishing Path: Where you decide whether you want to pursue **Traditional Publishing**, go **Indie**, or shoot for the best of both worlds with a **Hybrid** approach.

Self-Publishing Pillar #2—Get a Brilliant Book Cover: Where you learn the importance of an attention-grabbing book cover that fits your genre.

Self-Publishing Pillar #3—Hire a Professional Editor: Where we talk about the different kinds of editing and why working with a **Professional Editor** is essential.

Self-Publishing Pillar #4—Format Your Book for Success: Where you learn about **Practical** and **Fancy** formatting, and how to make the inside of your book look good.

Self-Publishing Pillar #5—Perfect Your Product Description: Where you learn some blurb writing techniques.

Self-Publishing Pillar #6—Decide to Go Wide (or Stay Exclusive): Where we discuss the great exclusive vs. wide publishing debate.

Part 2: Wading into the Self-Publishing Pool

Self-Publishing Pillar #7—Platforms, Metadata, and Hitting Publish: Where you discover how to upload your book to the major retailers and smash that publish button.

Self-Publishing Pillar #8—The Direct Route: Where we chat about selling directly to readers, and you decide whether it's right for you.

Part 3: Post-Publishing

Self-Publishing Pillar #9—The Call to Action: Where you ask your readers for a cheeky favour.

Self-Publishing Pillar #10—Your Website and Mailing List: Where we chat about owning your own space on the internet and the most powerful tool for reaching readers.

Self-Publishing Pillar #11—Content Marketing: Where you learn some free ways to market your books.

Self-Publishing Pillar #12—Social Media Marketing: Where we look at what using social media really means for authors.

Self-Publishing Pillar #13—Paid Advertising: Where you discover how to reach more readers by paying to get your books in front of people.

What This Book Isn't

Let me be clear.

This is not a book about the craft of writing, and it won't teach you how to write a novel. If you want to learn more about the writing craft, you can check out the other books in the *Write Better Fiction* series:

- *How to Write Brilliant Beginnings: Crafting Your Novel's Opening Chapters Made Easy*
- *How to Plot Your Novel: Outlining for Authors Made Easy*
- *How to Write Novels Fast: Productivity for Authors Made Easy*
- *How to Edit Your Novel: Self-Revisions for Authors Made Easy*

As I mentioned in the **Introduction**, some people view **Independent Publishing** as an inferior option, with **Traditional Publishing** being the one true path to writerly greatness.

That said, this book isn't:

- A treaty on why one type of publishing is better than the other (neither is better nor worse, they're just different)
- A way to slam **Traditionally Published Authors** for "selling-out" or "taking the simple route" (pursuing trad-pub isn't easy and comes with its own set of hurdles to jump)
- An exhaustive guide to marketing your book (I've included some things I do to market my books in the marketing section, but targeted books and courses about marketing are out there)

Okay... Rant Over

In each chapter, I'll break down how I've used **The Thirteen Pillars of Self-Publishing** in my author career, and how you can use them too.

I also mention some of my favourite free (and paid) **Self-Publishing Resources** throughout.

You'll notice I highlight certain terms in **Bold**, like this. This is intentional, because they're things I want you to remember.

I'll also pose questions for you to consider along the way. Answer these questions, and by the time we've finished, you'll have a published book you can hold in your hand (and/or upload to your e-reader).

Right.

That's enough introductory waffling on from me.

You cracked open this guide to learn **How to Publish Your Novel**.

So, let's get into it!

DISCLAIMER!

Oh.

Before we do...

A quick **Disclaimer**.

When I wrote the first draft of this book, I littered it (smothered it, actually), with the phrase, "at the time of writing". It felt repetitive and dull, and that's the last thing I want this book to be.

So, I'll say it up front, and say it once.

While most of the advice in *How to Publish Your Book*, is evergreen, there are resources and processes I mention that might change over time, particularly, the costs of certain paid services.

When you research platforms, pricing, or similar, please note these things could change over time (as much as I'd love to set these prices forever, I don't have that power).

Part 1: Pre-Publishing Prep

Where you pick your publishing path, get your novel camera ready, and deal with distribution.

Self-Publishing Pillar #1

Pick Your Publishing Path

"You don't need to ask anyone's permission to write or publish."

—Joanna Penn, Successful Self-Publishing

Obviously, I'm going to be placing a heavy emphasis on **Independent Publishing** throughout this book, because it's the path I chose when I threw my hat into the writing ring, and the one I'm most familiar with.

That doesn't mean it's the only way to publish, and it doesn't mean it'll be the best way for you to publish.

Broadly speaking, there are three ways to publish:

- **Traditional Publishing**
- **Independent Publishing**

- **Hybrid Publishing**

Let's look at each of these, so you can work out which might suit you best.

What is Traditional Publishing?

Traditional Publishing is where you aim to sell the **Intellectual Property Rights** for your book and/or series to a **Traditional Publishing House**.

This process usually involves pitching your book to an agent, who pitches it to acquisition editors at publishing houses. If the publishing house likes your book, and they agree to publish it, the agent takes a cut of your lifetime royalties (usually 10%-15%) in exchange for their services.

Caution

A reputable agent shouldn't charge any upfront fees to work with you. Their payment comes in the form of the royalty split I mentioned. Equally, a publishing house shouldn't charge you to actually publish your book.

If you find yourself in either of these situations, recognise the gargantuan red flags and run for the hills (or find another agent and publisher).

Note

Sometimes, an agent isn't necessary if you pitch to small presses who accept submission directly from authors.

The Pros of Traditional Publishing

There are many pros to **Traditional Publishing,** which still make it an attractive option for many authors. These include (but aren't limited to):

- **Prestige:** If you've always dreamed of having the *Penguin* logo on your novel's spine, and this is non-negotiable, then pursuing **Trad-Pub** could be the right option for you.

- **Access to Literary Awards:** A good few literary awards (although not all of them) still refuse to accept **Indie-Published** novels. Is winning a literary award something you want to achieve? If so, start looking for an agent.

- **Access to Bestseller Lists:** With a **Traditional Publisher** (and the required number of sales) backing you, you stand a chance of securing spots on *The New York Times, Sunday Times, and USA Today* bestseller lists, resulting in greater exposure for your work.

- **Your Team Supplied for You:** When you work with a **Traditional Publisher,** they bring their own team of cover designers, editors, proofreaders, etc. onto the project, at no cost to you. This is one of the big draws of signing a **Trad** deal.

- **The Advance:** When publishers pay an advance, this means they pay you a pre-arranged sum of money up front to buy the rights to your book.

- **Marketing:** If you're lucky, the publisher will supply you with a marketing budget, and might even give your book an advertising push at launch to spread the word.

- **Leveraging Intellectual Property Rights:** Some publishers will leverage your **Intellectual Property Rights** for you, producing your book in all formats (eBook, Paperback, Hardback, and Audio) and, if the book sells particularly well, can also broker deals to sell TV and movie rights, which (although rare in the grand scheme of things) could prove lucrative.

The Cons of Traditional Publishing

I once heard indie-author and podcaster, J. Thorn, talk about a writer's publishing choices in a way that made sense to me. I'm paraphrasing here, but regarding **Traditional Publishing**, he said something like, "You can't choose to **Traditionally Publish**, you can only choose to pursue **Traditional Publishing**."

Boom!

Mind officially blown.

Publishers sift through a lot of manuscripts when deciding which authors they want to back, and there's no guarantee one of the big boys will pick you.

That said, let's take a peek at the cons of **Traditional Publishing**:

- **It's a Lottery:** You have to be one of the chosen ones to find success in the **Trad-Pub** world.

- **It takes time:** When you sell your book to a **Traditional Publisher,** you'll likely wait a long time until they actually publish your book. It will need to go through multiple rounds of editing, the cover design team will take the cover through a ton of iterations, and the marketing team will need to decide how best to pitch your book to readers.

- **The advance:** While an advance might seem attractive (who wouldn't want a lump sum of money?) the way it's paid out might not. Say your publisher pays you an advance of $25,000. That's good, right? Yeah, but you won't receive it all at once. You'll likely receive a portion on submission. A portion after the editing rounds, and a portion after publication, which will take some time.

- **The royalties:** The royalty rate paid to the author is somewhere between 10% and 15% of each sale on average. Even if your publisher prices your eBook at $9.99, that doesn't leave much loose change at the end. Also, remember you won't start receiving royalty payouts until your book has "earned out" (or until your book has earned enough to pay back your advance).

- **The Lack of Control:** Depending on your personality type, this might not bother you, but (mostly) **Traditionally Published** authors have very little say in things like cover design, marketing and—sometimes—editorial decisions.

What is Independent Publishing?

Independent Publishing is where you keep all the **Intellectual Property Rights** to your books, and choose to **Self-Publish** on the various online retail stores, like:

- Amazon
- Kobo
- Google Play
- Apple Books
- Third party aggregators like *Draft2Digital*, which handle distribution to smaller stores and/or stores authors can't access directly
- Provided you're not signed up to Amazon's exclusive **KDP Select** program (more on this later), you can also sell your eBooks direct to readers through your website, or a hosted online store (more on this later, too).

Independent Publishing also means sourcing your own cover designers, editors, and proofreaders (at personal financial cost), and working with them to produce a quality product readers will enjoy.

The Pros of Independent Publishing

All the **Publishing Paths,** have many pros, including **Independent Publishing**. These include (but aren't limited to):

- **Greater Control:** You're in complete control of your publishing empire. You get to choose which cover designers and editors you work with, and get to make all the decisions on how the final product turns out.

- **Greater Flexibility:** What if the cover trends in your genre shift, and a new design (totally different from your current cover) becomes the "in thing"? You can change that. It's simply a matter of contacting your cover designer and filling out a new design brief. As soon as you've got your updated cover, you can switch out the old one, and avert any cover crises.

- **Higher Royalties:** Royalty payments are much higher than those you can expect from a **Traditional Publisher**. Take Amazon, for example. If you price your book between $2.99 and $9.99, the royalty rate is 70% per sale. If you price your book below $2.99 or above $9.99, the royalty rate drops to 35%, which is still higher than the average **Trad-Pub** deal.

- **Freedom to Pivot:** What happens if you're three books deep into a ten-book series, and you know it isn't going anywhere? You can pivot. Use book four to wrap up any dangling plot threads (you don't want to annoy readers who enjoy the series by leaving big questions unanswered) and move on to the next shiny new project.

- **Freedom to choose:** You get to choose which rights you keep and which ones you sell. For instance, producing human-narrated audiobooks can be bloody expensive. Rather than paying a narrator (or opting for a royalty-split deal between you and the narrator), you could decide to pursue an **Audio-Only Publishing Deal** with a **Traditional Publisher**.

- **More Sales Channels:** If your eBooks are **Wide** (not in **KDP Select**) you can sell directly to readers through your website or a hosted online store. The advantage here is you only pay transaction fees, and can keep over 90% of the royalties per sale.

Caution

Signing up to Amazon Kindle's **KDP Select** program with eBooks means you can only sell your eBooks on Amazon. You can't sell them through any other online retailer, aggregator, or direct from your website, because that's against Amazon's terms of service. And don't even think about breaking those terms... it's a serious no-no.

Note

You **CAN** still sell your print books through other retailers, aggregators, and direct through your website (using a **Print On Demand** service like Lulu Xpress, or Book Vault).

The Cons of Independent Publishing

I'm going to say this up-front, because I don't want anyone to make the starry-eyed decision to **Indie-Publish** based on the higher royalties and greater creative control.

While those things are fantastic, and a huge part of the reason I chose to be an **Indie-Author**, it's bloody hard work. You're responsible for everything, and I don't just mean the creative decision making. You're also responsible for all the admin, advertising, marketing, and promotion. When you **Indie-Publish** (if your goal is to make money from your writing), you are running a small business, and the buck stops with you.

With that in mind, let's delve into the cons of **Indie-Publishing**:

- **It's all on you:** Every decision rests with you. If you mess something up, you've only got yourself to blame. This can feel like an enormous responsibility, and you need to decide whether all the pros outweigh this con.

- **It takes effort:** Apart from the independent contractors you hire to assist with cover design and editing; you need to wear all the hats. As I mentioned above, you're the author, marketer, advertiser, publisher, social media manager (if social media is part of your marketing effort), PR person, and... and... and... honestly, this list never ends.

- **Find the right team:** Finding reliable contractors to assist you on your author journey can be tough. I'm truly blessed to have a stellar team around me I can count on to produce results, but that's not always the case. It takes a lot of searching to get the right people in your corner.

- **It can be insular (if you let it):** There are no fancy meetings with your publisher and marketing team, or glitzy events and book launches (unless you pay for them yourself), so this path can feel isolating. My top tip to combat this is to join writing communities that support your needs and goals. I'm a member of multiple author cohorts (each one of which gets mentioned in the Acknowledgements section of all my books), because I couldn't do this without them. I can't emphasise how important it is to find like-minded writers you can hang with (either virtually or in person) to make this journey easier.

- **Finding readers is hard:** Which is why I'm so grateful for mine (yes, that means you, too!). It bears repeating, but it's all on you, including finding readers. Sometimes you feel like the loon on the street corner, with a megaphone and a sandwich board, yelling, "BUY MY BOOK!" into the void, with no response (All jokes aside: please don't repeatedly ask people to buy your book, it's annoying—more on this in the **Marketing Section**).

What is Hybrid Publishing?

Hybrid Publishing is where:

- You have some **Traditionally Published** books and/or series, and some **Independently Published** books and/or series, or

- You sell certain **Intellectual Property Rights** to a **Traditional Publisher** (think by format, like an **Audio-Only Traditional** deal) and keep others as an **Independent Publisher**.

The Pros of Hybrid Publishing

The two major pros of **Hybrid Publishing** are:

- **Access to hard-to-produce formats:** I know a few authors who are **Hybrid Published** for **Foreign Language Rights**, meaning that they've signed **Translation Rights** over to a publisher to produce their books in other languages, something that is notoriously difficult for **Indie-Authors** to accomplish on their own.

- **Best of both worlds:** You can access things only open to **Traditionally Published Authors** (awards, bestseller lists, etc.) with your **Trad-Pub** titles, while still keeping full creative control over your **Independently Published** work.

The Cons of Hybrid Publishing

The major con of **Hybrid Publishing** is:

- **It's double the work:** You'll need to work with your publisher to manage your **Traditionally Published** titles and **Rights**, and do everything an **Indie-Author** does to manage their **Independently Published** portfolio.

Final Thoughts on Picking Your Publishing Path

Choosing how you want to publish isn't easy. I'm hoping that by outlining the pros and cons of each approach, you can make an educated guess about what you want to do with your **Intellectual Property**.

Questions to Consider

- Knowing what you know now about **Traditional Publishing**, is this a **Publishing Path** you want to pursue?
- What steps do you need to take to give yourself the best chance of success in the **Traditional Publishing** world?
- Knowing what you know now about **Independent Publishing**, is this a **Publishing Path** you want to pursue?
- What steps do you need to take to give yourself the best chance of success in the **Indie-Publishing** world?
- Knowing what you know now about **Hybrid Publishing**, is this a **Publishing Path** you want to pursue?
- What steps do you need to take to give you the best chance

of success in the **Hybrid Publishing** world?

SELF-PUBLISHING PILLAR #2

GET A BRILLIANT BOOK COVER

"With an unprofessional cover, or a cover that doesn't immediately communicate the benefits, readers will never read the description of your book. They won't know what it's about or whether they might like it."
—Derek Murphy, Book Cover Design Secrets You Can Use to Sell More Books

HOLD UP, SHANE! WHAT in the name of all things bookish do you mean when you say, "Get a brilliant book cover?"

You're killing it with these questions.

If you looked at the three **Self-Publishing Paths** in the previous chapter:

- **Traditional Publishing**

- **Independent Publishing**
- **Hybrid Publishing**

And decided **Indie-Publishing** was your jam, then it's on you to make sure your book is camera ready (or that it looks enticing enough for readers to buy).

How you package and present your book is just as important as its content (especially if you want your novel to sell).

Self-Publishing Pillars 2 – 5 focus on the things you need to do to present your book well. These are:

- **Self-Publishing Pillar #2—Get a Brilliant Cover:** Does the cover you've chosen fit with your book's genre, and what readers expect to see?

- **Self-Publishing Pillar #3—Hire a Professional Editor:** Have you had your book professionally edited? Does the story shine, does your prose pack a punch, and have you eliminated all possible spelling and grammar errors?

- **Self-Publishing Pillar #4—Format for Success:** Have you formatted (or sourced a professional to format) your book in a way that makes its interior attractive? If you've read my book, *How to Write Brilliant Beginnings*, you know how important a novel's opening chapters are (this extends to the way they look when a reader downloads a free sample).

- **Self-Publishing Pillar #5—Perfect Your Product Description:** Have you written an engaging **Book Description** you can use on the back of your print books (and on the online retail stores) that hooks readers in and makes them want to buy your book?

Let's start with the outside of your book and look at all things **Cover Design**.

Getting a Brilliant Book Cover

Getting the cover designed for my next novel is one of my favourite parts of the publishing process. There's nothing like getting the email from your cover designer with the initial design concepts attached. I get such a buzz from this because the book feels real.

Some common questions newer writer's ask me about cover design are:

- How do I know what needs to go on my cover?
- How do I find a cover designer to work with?
- What do they need me to tell them to produce a brilliant design?
- How much will it cost?
- What if I'm not happy with the result?

So, let's do a deep dive into all things cover design.

How do I know what needs to go on my cover?

Working out what elements you might like to include on your cover can be tricky.

The first thing you need to do is identify your novel's genre. Are you writing a:

- Romance
- Sci-fi
- Fantasy
- Young Adult Dystopian
- Horror
- Thriller

Or something else?

Once you know what genre you're writing in, it's time to don your **Market Research** hat and get to work.

Go to Amazon (or your preferred book retailer of choice) and find the bestseller list for your genre. Scan the top 100 in that list, and see if you can identify any common:

- Colours (e.g., thrillers use a lot of yellows and blues)

- Background types (e.g., urban fantasy covers usually have a city backdrop)
- Themes (e.g., do the covers feel dark and broody, or light and fun)
- Fonts (e.g., romance relies on swirly, decorative fonts)
- Foreground types (e.g., character, symbol, or setting)

This is exactly what I did when I was ready to have the cover designed for my debut novel, an urban fantasy thriller called *The Witch's Revenge.* I found a bestseller list for my genre and paid close attention to reoccurring patterns. For example:

- **Independently Published** urban fantasy books favour covers featuring characters wearing leather jackets, staring (or glaring) straight into the camera.
- They have backgrounds featuring urban areas, usually pictured at nighttime.
- The character usually has "hand farts", or some kind of magical energy spilling from their fingers.
- The book title fonts are bold and blocky, or decorative yet spiky.
- The other fonts (author and series name) are plain and contemporary.
- The author's name usually appears at the top of the page.
- The book title usually appears in the bottom third of the

page, beneath the character.

- The series name usually appears in the smallest font, beneath the book title, right at the bottom of the page.

You'll find these common themes in any genre, and once you see all the covers together in a bestsellers list, they're pretty easy to identify.

Woah, woah, woah!

You're telling me my cover should look similar to everyone else's? If that's true, how the hell is my book going to stand out?

The truth is:

Your book will stand out (for the right reasons) if your cover looks similar to the bestselling covers in your genre.

Put it this way. If a romance reader went to the romance charts, and saw a cover with the "wrong" colours, background, themes, fonts, and foreground, what do you think they're going to do?

That's right.

They're going to think, "This book isn't for me," and move on.

There's a simple reason for this:

Genre = Reader Expectations

If you're marketing a thriller novel to thriller readers, they expect to see a cover that looks like the thrillers they know and love. If you're selling a sci-fi novel to sci-fi readers, you'd better make damn sure your cover gives them what they're expecting.

That's the thing about **Independent Publishing**. You might have skirted around the slush piles and gatekeepers of the **Traditional Publishing** world, but readers are your gatekeepers now.

I'm going to repeat that, just to hammer the point home.

Readers are your gatekeepers!

Give them what they expect and they're more likely to buy your books. Surprise them (in a bad way) with a cover that looks like it belongs somewhere else, and they'll skip your novel and move on to the next one.

I've warned you!

How do I find a cover designer to work with?

Not going to lie...

This is tough.

It took me a long time to find a cover designer I was happy with, because I knew how important cover design was to my book's success, and I wanted to get it right.

But how do you get it right when there are so many designers to choose from?

There are a few ways to make sure you aren't hiring a dud:

- **Ask for a recommendation:** If you know other authors who write in your genre, and you love their covers, reach out to them and ask who their cover designer is.

- **Check your favourite books:** If you read a book and think the cover is spot on, check the book's front matter, back matter, and/or Acknowledgements. Most authors give a shout-out to their cover designer somewhere.

- **Do an online search:** In your search engine of choice type **[your genre] + cover designer** and look at a few designer websites. If you choose this method, I'd recommend looking at the designer's portfolio to gauge whether their work matches what you're looking for, and see if they have a testimonials section, featuring reviews from satisfied customers.

- **Use a vetted list of designers:** Organisations like *Reedsy* and *The Alliance of Independent Authors* vet the designers they recommend and feature to make sure their work is up to standard. If you're a member of *The Alliance of Independent Authors,* you'll often get discounts on services purchased through one of their *Partner Members.*

What do they need me to tell them to produce a brilliant design?

When you contact a cover designer and ask them to work with you, they'll likely issue you with a design brief. You fill out the brief, clearly explaining what you want your designer to produce.

A Word of Warning!

Now is not the time to be vague.

Fill out the brief with as much specificity as possible. The more you give your cover designer to work with, the less likely you are to be disappointed with the result.

Here's a list of some things you can expect to see on a design brief:

PERSONAL INFORMATION

- Your name
- Your email address

ABOUT YOUR BOOK

- Book title
- Author name (or penname)
- Genre
- Brief description of the book
- Character description (if you want a character on your cover)
- Setting description (if you want a location on your cover as

the backdrop)

EXAMPLES

- Links to similar covers (even if your designer doesn't ask for this, I'd still send them links to 3-5 covers that you want to emulate, because it'll give them a clear idea of what you're looking for).

If you're getting a print cover designed (besides the eBook cover), the designer will also ask for:

PRODUCT DESCRIPTION

- Your book's product description (or blurb)

TRIM SIZE

This is the size you want your printed book to be. Popular **Trim Sizes** include:

- 5" x 8" (my preference)
- 5.5" x 8.5"
- 6" x 9"

But other sizes are available.

PAGE COUNT

- The number of pages in your **Print-Ready** (the file formatted for your print book's **Trim Size**) manuscript.

PAPER COLOUR

- Cream paper is slightly thinner and is a popular choice for fiction.
- White paper is slightly thicker and is a popular choice for non-fiction.
- Designers need to know the **Paper Colour** because the thickness of the paper affects the book's final spine width.

PUBLISHING PLATFORM

- The file specifications for the different **Print on Demand (POD)** services (like KDP Print and Ingram Spark differ slightly).

ISBN

- An **ISBN** is your book's **International Standard Book Number**, used by booksellers, online stores, libraries, publishers, etc. to identify your book (**NOTE:** If you use **ISBNs** for your eBooks, audiobooks, or any additional formats like large print, you'll need one **ISBN** per format).
- **A Brief Note on ISBNs: ISBNs** are free in certain countries (Canada is one such country), but in most places they cost money, and they're not cheap. Use a search engine to find the

ISBN distributor for your country.

What does cover design cost?

The honest answer is...

It depends.

Designers all charge different rates and as soon as I try to commit those to paper, they'll likely change. Rather than give specific pricing, let's talk about the type of covers you can buy, from the cheapest to the most expensive:

- **Pre-Made Covers:** The designer will have already added elements like background, foreground, title fonts and colour palette. When you buy a pre-made cover, the designer will simply add your book title and author name to the cover, and may make additional (small) tweaks on request.

- **Custom photo-manipulation covers:** These are probably the most common type of cover, where you submit a design brief and the designer purchases stock images and fonts to create the cover to your specification. The designer will manipulate the images in Photoshop (or similar) to produce the final product.

- **Custom illustrated covers:** Where a visual artist draws custom images for your cover (like a specific character, for example) and a photo-manipulation artist incorporates these illustrations (along with the fonts, etc.) into the finished design.

It won't surprise you that pre-made covers are the cheapest option and custom illustrated covers are the most expensive, because of the amount of work that goes into each type of design.

Consider what's best for you (and your budget) when choosing the type of cover you want. And remember, as an **Independent Publisher**, you can always buy a more expensive cover later if the book sells well, and you think it's worth it.

What if I'm not happy with the result?

If you filled out your design brief with enough detail, provided examples, and gave as many specifics as possible, this shouldn't happen.

But there's always a chance...

So, if the cover isn't to your liking, ask the designer whether they allow revisions (ideally, you'll have found this out in the researching phase). Most designers will allow a certain number of revisions, and some allow unlimited revisions (within reason).

Final Thoughts on Getting a Brilliant Book Cover

Despite what your great-great-aunt Ethel tells you, people (readers, specifically) *do* judge books by their covers...

And they're unforgiving.

If you have a brilliant book cover designed, you greatly increase the chances that readers will click on to your product page and read your book description.

Get a shoddy cover at your peril.

Questions to Consider

- Have you looked at the bestseller lists in your genre to identify common themes in cover design?
- If not, take some time to do that now.
- Have you found a cover designer you want to work with?
- If not, how can you find one?
- Take some time to do that now.

SELF-PUBLISHING PILLAR #3

HIRE A PROFESSIONAL EDITOR

"It's important to always check the terms and conditions of your editor's website and make sure you're clear about the type of edit you're getting and what's included."
—Sacha Black, The Anatomy of Prose

I COVER THIS TOPIC in *How to Edit Your Novel: Self-Revisions for Authors Made Easy*, but I'll include a summary of what to expect from the **Professional Editing Process** here.

Much like with cover design, it's a good idea, when sourcing an editor to work with, to:

- Ask for recommendations
- Look at well-written books and see if the author mentions their editor

- Do an online search for an editor
- Use a vetted list of editors (again, check out places like *Reedsy* and *The Alliance of Independent Authors)* for lists of vetted editors

The most common question writers ask me around **Professional Editing** is, "What type of edit do I need, and how much will it cost?"

That very much depends on your goals for the book, but I've broken down the most common editing packages out there so you can make an educated decision about which one to choose:

- **Beta-Reading:** You can source paid or free beta readers to read your book and tell you where they stopped reading, got bored, got irritated with a character, etc. before sending your book to a professional editor. This will be at the cheapest end of the scale if you're using a paid beta reader.
- **Developmental Editing:** This is where you hire a **Professional Editor** to provide positive and constructive feedback on elements of your story like story arc, character, plot, setting, and pacing, etc. These editing packages are expensive, but well worth the investment.
- **Line/Copyediting:** Where you hire a **Professional Editor** to examine your prose and sentence structure to make sure they shine.
- **Proofreading:** Where you hire a **Proofreader** to pick out any typos, grammatical errors, or weird sentence constructions.

What are you saying? That I have to hire each of these people to carry out every type of edit on my book? I'm not made of money, pal!

No.

That's not what I'm saying, and I get where you're coming from. In an ideal world—where money grows on trees and pigs fly—it would be awesome to run your book through each of these stages (that's what a **Traditional Publisher** would do for you, right?).

But, 99.99999% of **Indie-Authors**—me included—work with tight budgets, and have to be smart about where they invest their money.

Because that's what editing is...

An investment.

Part of getting your book camera ready is having it **Professionally Edited**. People often ask me whether they really need to hire an editor, or whether they can get by without one.

Here's my answer:

I'm a developmental editor, and I still hire a developmental editor when I write novels.

Why?

Because I'm too close to the story. It's impossible for me to examine my story arc, characters, plot, pacing, etc. myself. I will miss something, and the book will suck.

Am I saying everyone needs a developmental editor?

No.

I'm saying that's the type of edit I need, because telling a great story is the most important thing to me.

It might be different for you. Perhaps you can tell a solid story, and only need to use **Beta Readers** to tighten things up. Maybe it's the **Copyediting** where you need help, or maybe **Proofreading** is a must for you, because you know you always miss those pesky typos.

So, no, I'm not saying you absolutely must have a certain type of edit. I am saying you should have some kind of **Professional Edit**.

But what if I can't afford it?

Trust me, I hear you, and I don't believe anyone's socio-economic status should prohibit them from publishing. One of the best pieces of advice I can give if you genuinely can't afford a **Professional Editor** (the same goes for a **Cover Designer** too), is to offer a **Skill Swap.**

What's a Skill Swap?

A **Skill Swap** is where you offer to carry out a task, project, or piece of work for the person you want to hire in exchange for their services. Have a think about the things you're good at that you could offer. Maybe you crush:

- Admin work

- Graphic design
- Website design
- Social media marketing

Whatever it is, ask if you can do some work for the designer or editor in exchange for the project you want them to carry out.

It might surprise you how many people are open to this. The thing you're good at and love could be the thing they're bad at and hate doing.

Final Thoughts on Hiring a Professional Editor

Of all the things you need to do before **Independently Publishing** your book, getting a cracking cover and a **Professional Edit** are essential. As soon as you put your book up for sale, you're asking readers to part with their hard-earned cash.

That said, you owe it to them to produce the best quality work you can.

Questions to Consider

- Have you decided which type (or types) of **Professional Edit** you need?
- If not, where could you best spend this investment: on the story, the prose, or the last-minute errors?
- Have you found a **Professional Editor** you want to work with yet?
- If not, how can you find one?
- Take some time to do that now.

SELF-PUBLISHING PILLAR #4

FORMAT YOUR BOOK FOR SUCCESS

"When done properly, well-chosen front and back matter will help readers distinguish your carefully crafted, professional-looking, self-published book from the others on the shelf who have half-assed their efforts and skipped over this entirely."

—Daniel Willcocks, The Self-Publishing Blueprint

THERE ARE TWO THINGS you need to consider when formatting:

- **Practical Formatting**
- **Fancy Formatting**

Wait! What's the difference?

I'm glad you asked.

What is Practical Formatting?

This is the order you place things in your novel. For instance, do you know where your **Also By** page should sit? Do your **Acknowledgements** come before or after the story? Where does the **Dedication** go again?

Getting your front and back matter in the right order is vital, because it'll make your book look professional. The key (if you're **Independently Publishing**) is to make your books indistinguishable from their **Trad-Pub** counterparts.

Readers have high expectations, and we don't want to disappoint. Here's how I **Practically Format** my books:

FRONT MATTER

- **Title page:** Featuring the book's title, subtitle or series title, and publishing imprint (the imprint name you choose to publish under—I publish my books under Tagline Publishing).
- **Also By Page:** Where you list any other books you've published (preferably in order if writing in a series)
- **Copyright Page:** Where you list the copyright information from your book

- **Table of Contents:** Optional for fiction, but necessary for non-fiction
- **Trigger Warnings:** Some authors choose to include trigger warnings in their novels if they deal with sensitive, or upsetting themes (you can find an example of a **Trigger Warning** in the front matter of N. L. Blandford's dark crime thriller, *The Perilous Road to Her*)
- **Dedication:** Where you dedicate the book to whomever you choose
- **Epigraph:** Where you include an attributed quote that ties into the theme of the book (for example, I used a quote from Joseph Alexander's *Self-Published Millionaire* as the **Epigraph** for this book)
- **Foreword:** If another author writes a **Foreword** to your book, then this is where it goes (this is more common in non-fiction than fiction).

MAIN BODY

- **The Novel Itself:** This is where you put the book's main content

BACK MATTER

- **Afterword:** This is the same as (and used instead of) a **Foreword** (again, it's more common in non-fiction than fiction).
- **Call to Action (or CTA):** Where you ask the reader to do

something for you. This could be to leave a review, join your mailing list, buy the next book in the series, etc. The beauty of being **Independently Published** is that you can change your **CTAs** depending on what you need readers to do.

- **Acknowledgements:** Where you give your writerly Oscars speech and thank everyone who helped you bring your literary love child into being
- **About the Author:** Where you include a snazzy headshot, your author bio, and links to your website and social media pages.
- **References:** Where you include attribution to any other books, websites, articles, etc. you've quoted in your book.
- **Also By Page:** I include this at the very front and very back of my books

So, that's your **Practical Formatting** taken care of.

What about **Fancy Formatting**?

What is Fancy Formatting?

This is the fun bit (at least for me).

It's where you get to choose how your:

- Chapter headings
- Chapter subtitles
- Ornamental breaks (the little motifs in between scenes)

Look when someone's reading your book.

There are a ton of free (and paid) formatting options.

Free Options

When I first started out, I didn't have any book formatting software, because I was working on a tight budget, so I had to look for free options that would do a professional job.

My favourite free option is *Draft2Digital's* book formatting tool. It's really simple to use, and you can produce an attractive eBook in as little as five minutes.

You just enter your book's details, upload your manuscript in a docx format, upload your cover, check your chapter headings are correct, choose one of the pre-made (genre-specific) formatting themes, and download the publish-ready files in the various formats.

It's that easy!

The best part is, you don't even have to distribute the book through *Draft2Digital* to use the tool. How cool is that?

If *D2D* isn't your thing, then *Reedsy* has a free book formatting tool, and there are other options out there, too.

Paid Options

There are two major players in the book formatting space:

- **Vellum:** This is a Mac only piece of software (although Windows users can get access through Mac-in-Cloud) and provides a quick and easy way to format books with a great deal of control. Vellum offers eBook only formatting (flat fee of £169.99 GBP), or eBook and paperback formatting (flat fee of £209.99 GBP).

- **Atticus:** This is cloud based (so works on PC or Mac) and is my preferred option. You can select pre-made templates, design your own and (if you have a paid Book Brush account), create your own ornamental breaks and custom chapter headings. Atticus is available for a flat fee of $147.00 USD for eBook and Paperback formatting.

Final Thoughts on Formatting Your Book for Success

If you want your book to be the full package, it's worth investing either time or money into formatting it properly, depending on your patience for learning new skills, or your budget.

Having a well-formatted book gives your book that professional edge readers will appreciate.

Questions to Consider

- Have you decided whether to outsource **Formatting**, or do it yourself?
- If you're outsourcing, have you found a **Formatter** you want to work with?
- If not, how can you find one?
- Take some time to do that now.
- If you're **Formatting** yourself, do you know which free (or paid) formatting tool you want to use?
- If not, take some time to do that now.

SELF-PUBLISHING PILLAR #5

PERFECT YOUR PRODUCT DESCRIPTION

*"Believe it or not, effective book packaging actually combines three equally crucial components: title, cover and pitch [or **Product Description**]."*
—Libbie Hawker, Gotta Read It!

WHETHER YOU CHOOSE TO write your **Product Description** yourself, or hire someone to write it for you, it's the last essential ingredient for making your book ready for the big wide world.

It's your **Product Description's** job to sell your book, and the aim is to hook your reader in so they can't refuse clicking that buy button.

The **Product Description** can make or break a book's chances of success. If you can't sell a reader on your book's premise, they skedaddle off your product page and give their money to A. N. Other-Author.

Let's take a peek at:

- **Fiction Product Descriptions**
- **Non-fiction Product Descriptions**

6 Top Tips for Writing a Fantastic Fiction Product Description

Here are my **6 Top Tips for Writing a Fantastic Fiction Product Description**.

Tip #1: Start with a Hook

Much like the opening line of your novel, the aim of your **Product Description Hook** is to peak your reader's interest and keep them reading.

One of the most famous product description hooks in the **Indie-Author** space comes from Adam Croft's thriller, *Her Last Tomorrow.*

Here's the hook:

"Could you murder your wife to save your daughter?"
—Adam Croft, Her Last Tomorrow

If that isn't gripping, I don't know what is!

Opening a **Book Description** with a hook like this is a surefire way to keep readers reading.

Tip #2: Introduce Your Protagonist

Your protagonist is the character you want readers to connect with. That said, it's important you introduce them right off the bat, and provide an interesting detail or two about their personality.

A good example of **Protagonist Introduction** in a **Book Description** comes from Brad Magnarella's urban fantasy novel, *Demon Moon*:

"Everson Croft, professor of mythology and behind-the-scenes wizard."
—Brad Magnarella, Demon Moon

I wouldn't necessarily use the protagonist's title or last name in a **Book Description**, unless you're writing a crime thriller introducing Detective Joe Blogs, or something similar, because too many details in **Book Descriptions** weigh readers down.

Tip #3: Introduce the Everyday World

If you've read any of my other non-fiction books, you'll know all about **The Everyday World**. It's where your protagonist starts their story, and where they are the most **Scarred** (flawed).

For example, in my **Book Description** for *The Witch's Revenge*, I introduce Henry's everyday world like this:

> *"Henry had everything a twenty-one-year-old could want. A degree, a loving family, awesome friends to chill with, and a bright future..."*
> **—S. W. Millar, The Witch's Revenge**

Tip #4: Raise the Stakes

In your novels, you disrupt your protagonist's status quo with a **Grenade** (Inciting Incident), and you need to do the same thing in your blurbs.

I finish the above line of *The Witch's Revenge* **Product Description** like this:

> *"Until that night destroyed his life. Now there's only one thing he wants."*
> **—S. W. Millar, The Witch's Revenge**

Tip #5: Introduce Obstacles

You need to tell the reader what is standing in your protagonist's way.

This **Obstacle Introduction** comes from *Dark Pawn*, a young adult urban fantasy novel by J. P. Rindfleisch and A. B. Cohen.

Here it is:

> *"It [the truth] lies in her mother's past. One with mysterious ties to a secret society of demon hunting mystics. Can she trust them to teach her what she needs to know, or will she just become another pawn in their game?"*
> **—J. P. Rindfleisch and A. B. Cohen, Dark Pawn**

It's clear from this **Obstacle Introduction** the kind of conflict the protagonist (Leah Ackerman) will face.

Tip #6: End with a Call to Action

You want your reader to buy your book once they've read your stellar **Product Description**. They're more likely to smash that buy button if you tell them to do it.

The best example of a call to action I've seen comes from Brian Meek's book on writing **Product Descriptions**, *Mastering Amazon Descriptions*.

Here's the formula:

> *"You'll love this [type of novel] because [reason]*
> *Get it now."*
> **—Brian Meeks, Mastering Amazon Descriptions**

I end the book description for the fourth novel in my *Myth & Magic* series, *The Demon's Shadow*, like this:

> *"You'll enjoy this gritty urban fantasy novel, because everyone loves a witch vs demon showdown and a sibling with secrets.*
> *Get it now."*
> **—S. W. Millar, The Demon's Shadow**

4 Top Tips for Writing a Knockout Non-fiction Product Description

Some of my tips for **Writing a Knockout Non-fiction Product Description** mirror those I use to write fiction blurbs, but there are some key differences. With fiction, you're trying to sell the protagonist's journey.

With non-fiction, you're trying to solve a problem.

Here are my **4 Top Tips for Writing a Knockout Non-fiction Product Description**:

Tip #1: Start with a Hook

Whether you're writing fiction or non-fiction, you still need to hook your reader in.

Here's an example of a non-fiction hook from Joanna Penn's *How to Write a Novel*:

"Writing a novel will change your life."
—Joanna Penn, How to Write a Novel

This hook works because it creates an **Invisible Question** in the reader's mind. Upon reading this, readers will immediately ask themselves, "How will writing a novel change my life?" and want to read on.

Tip #2: Introduce the Problem

Remember, you're trying to solve a problem for the reader. The reader needs to know what that problem is to know whether your book is for them.

This example comes from the **Product Description** for *Three Story Method* by J. Thorn and Zach Bohannon.

Here it is:

"Do you have an amazing idea for a novel but you struggle to get the words on the page?"
—J. Thorn and Zach Bohannon, Three Story Method

The problem here is clear.

Tip #3: Introduce the Solution

Tell the reader what your book will teach them, then bullet point the solutions your book provides.

This is the easiest way to **Introduce the Solution**.

Tip #4: End with a Call to Action

Just like with **Fiction Product Descriptions**, you want to tell your reader to buy, and get them to take action.

Here's a reminder of Brian Meek's **Call to Action** formula:

> *"You'll love this [type of book] because [reason]*
> *Get it now."*
> **—Brian Meeks, Mastering Amazon Descriptions**

I end the book description for the third writing guide in my *Write Better Fiction* series, *How to Write Novels Fast*, like this:

> *"You'll enjoy this handy guide to productivity because everyone loves an easy-to-follow process that produces results.*
> *Get it now."*
> **—Shane Millar, How to Write Novels Fast**

It's beyond this book to cover writing **Product Descriptions** in depth. If you want to delve further into this topic, then I highly recommend the books below:

- *How to Write a Sizzling Synopsis* by Bryan Cohen
- *Gotta Read It* by Libbie Hawker
- *Mastering Amazon Descriptions* by Brian D. Meeks

What is it with guys named Bryan/Brian writing how to books on blurbs...?

I'll ponder that another time.

Final Thoughts on Perfecting Your Product Description

Writing a killer **Product Description** is one of the best ways to convince readers to buy your book...

But a lackluster **Product Description** isn't going to convince anyone.

Follow the tips I've given you in this chapter, and you'll be well on your way to making more sales.

So, that's cover design, professional editing, formatting, and **Product Descriptions** ticked off the list.

See?

I told you there were a lot of hats involved if you chose the **Independent Publishing** route (so I hope you've got a big enough hat stand, my friend) but stick with me here...

I promise, the rewards are well worth it.

What's next on the agenda?

We're going to tackle one of the most controversial topics in modern publishing... yeah, I'm going to leave that hanging.

Questions to Consider

- In terms of your **Product Description**, are you going to write it yourself, or hire someone to do it for you?
- If you're doing it yourself, have you used the **Top Tips** in this chapter to give your **Product Description** a stellar structure?
- If you're outsourcing it, how are you going to find someone who can do it for you?

Self-Publishing Pillar #6

Decide to Go Wide (or Stay Exclusive)

"When you publish your books, you essentially have two primary publication options that are dictated by the kinds of places you choose to publish, and the methods by which you wish to sell your books."
—Daniel Willcocks, The Self-Publishing Blueprint

Before we get into the specifics of how to load your book onto the various online retail stores, I'm going to tackle one of the most contentious issues in the **Independent Publishing Community**.

Takes deep breath...

That's right, folks!

We're going to have a little chat about **Exclusive** versus **Wide Distribution**.

Say what now?

What's all this **Exclusive** versus **Wide** nonsense, and what's it got to do with me?

Let me explain.

What is Exclusive Distribution?

Exclusive Distribution is the term used when you enroll your eBook in Amazon's **KDP Select** program. When you enroll an eBook (or series of eBooks) in **Select**, you <u>**CANNOT**</u> sell it on any of the other online retailers, or via a virtual storefront on your website.

NOTE: I repeated the word "eBook" on purpose. **KDP Select's Exclusivity** terms only apply to eBooks. You can still sell your print books through multiple retailers or direct from your store.

What is KDP Select and How Does it Work?

These are the broad strokes on all things **KDP Select**:

- Enrollment is free to authors
- Once enrolled, Amazon makes your eBook available to **Kin-**

dle Unlimited customers (who pay a monthly subscription to borrow eBooks for free)

- Every time a customer actually reads (not borrows, but reads) your eBook, you get paid based on the number of pages they read
- The amount an author gets paid (per page read) fluctuates a little each month
- Once enrolled, you agree to keep your eBook in **KDP Select** for 90 days (you can automatically re-enroll at the end of this period—for another 90 days—or pull the eBook out)
- Customers who don't have a **Kindle Unlimited** subscription can still buy your eBook from Amazon in the usual way

Hang on, hang on!

If being enrolled in **KDP Select** means I can't sell my book anywhere else, why the hell would I want to do that?

Great question!

Let's look at the prose of **Exclusivity**.

The Pros of KDP Select

Here are some of the good things about being a **KDP Select** author:

- If you're new to self-publishing, this can be a good place to start because you only have to manage one sales platform, one set of reports, and one set of royalty payments

- If your books are long enough (e.g., standard novel length) you can make good money (provided people are reading your books)

- You can make use of promotion tools only available to **KDP Select** authors

- This is anecdotal (because Amazon doesn't share this data), but the consensus in the author community is Amazon is more likely to promote an eBook enrolled in **KDP Select** once it gets borrows or sales

- Again, anecdotal, but it's also consensus that a **KDP Select** eBook is more likely to place higher in Amazon's category bestseller lists once it gets borrows or sales

What are the KDP Select Promotional Tools

Kindle Countdown Deals

This is where you put your eBook on sale ($0.99, for example) for a set amount of time. Amazon places a countdown timer on the eBook's product page to let customers know exactly how much longer the sale lasts.

The idea is the countdown clock motivates readers to buy because they won't want to miss out on this sweet, sweet deal.

Free Book Promotion

As the name suggests, you can make your book free for a limited period (to people outside of the **Kindle Unlimited** ecosystem) to entice them to download.

If you have later books in the series, the hope is readers will love book 1 so much; they buy book 2, and so on.

NOTE

- You can only use these tools on five days of each 90-day **KDP Select** term
- You can only use one type of promotion per 90-day **KDP Select** term

Okay.

These are the benefits of enrolling an eBook in **KDP Select**.

What are the cons?

The Cons of KDP Select

Here are some reasons you might decide not to enroll your eBook in **KDP Select**:

- I mentioned this up top, but you can't sell your eBook anywhere else, which means it's only available to Amazon customers (you can't reach readers who use other devices, like Kobo customers, for instance)
- You're reliant on Amazon for all your eBook income: If

you're trying to run a business, you might not want to be reliant on one platform for the lion's share of your royalties (what if Amazon goes bust one day?)

- You can't sell your eBook direct through your website: Which means you can't take advantage of keeping over 90% of the royalties from your book sales

A Quick Note on Exclusivity vs. Subscription Programs

I want you to remember being **Exclusive** to Amazon doesn't mean every eBook subscription program demands **Exclusivity**.

Take Kobo's eBook subscription offering, **Kobo Plus**, for example. **Wide** authors (authors who aren't **Exclusive** to Amazon with their eBooks) can enroll in **Kobo Plus** and still sell their eBooks elsewhere.

Do your research before enrolling in any subscription program, so you know exactly what you're getting yourself into.

Okay.

That covers **Exclusive Distribution**.

What about **Wide Distribution**?

What is Wide Distribution?

Wide Distribution is when you don't enroll your eBook into Amazon's **KDP Select** program, which allows you to sell your eBook across multiple retailers, including:

- Amazon
- Kobo
- Apple Books
- Google Play Books
- Barnes & Noble
- Nook
- Aggregators (like *Draft 2 Digital*) to reach even more stores
- Direct from your website
- Library programs like *Scribd* and *Overdrive*

How Does Wide Distribution Work?

You open author accounts on some (or all) of the self-publishing platforms you can reach directly (*Kobo* is one such store) and use an aggregator site to distribute to stores you can't reach directly.

Let's look at some benefits of going **Wide**.

The Pros of Wide Distribution

- **Access to More Readers:** By publishing **Wide** you can reach readers on all the different stores (i.e., readers who don't own a Kindle or buy books from Amazon)
- **Direct Sales:** You can sell your eBooks direct from your website and earn much higher royalties from each sale
- **Access to Different Promotional Tools:** When you publish direct to stores like *Kobo*, *Apple Books*, or *Google Play Books*, you can take advantage of unique book promotion opportunities
- **A Broader Income Base:** One of the main arguments for going **Wide** is the fact you aren't reliant on one store (Amazon) for most of your book sales income (meaning that if Amazon went down the toilet, you'd still have money coming in from the other retailers)
- **Chance to Apply for a BookBub Featured Deal:** BookBub is a book promotion site that sends lists of free and discounted books to their tens of thousands of subscribers, and you pay to have your book featured (the catch is Bookbub are far more likely to feature **Wide** over **Exclusive** books—more on Bookbub in the **Marketing** section)
- **Ability to have Permafree eBooks:** If you want to use the first book in a series as a loss-leader (a product you give away for free to entice people to read further into the series), you can only do this by going **Wide** (when you set your book to

Permafree—$0.00—on the **Wide** stores, Amazon will price match, and your book will be free there, too)

The Cons of Wide Distribution

Now we've looked at the pros, let's chat about some reasons you might decide against going **Wide**:

- **Platform Management:** When you go wide, it's your job to manage each individual publishing platform you use (uploading all the book files, applying for various promotions across all the stores, reconciling royalty payments from multiple sources, etc.)
- **Reaching readers:** Reaching readers arguably takes more effort when you publish **Wide** (each platform has its own learning curve to convert readers into fans)
- **Time Management:** The more platforms you publish to, the longer it takes, so when you publish **Wide**, know that it will take you longer than going **Exclusive**, which is going to eat into your writing time

A Quick Note on Wide vs. Exclusive eBook Distribution

Let me be clear.

I have no beef with either **Exclusive** or **Wide** authors. The choice you make in terms of distribution will depend on your goals, the time you have to invest in your author business, and your tolerance for navigating multiple platforms.

REMEMBER!

It doesn't have to be all or nothing.

You can choose to enroll certain books (or series) in **KDP Select** and take other books (or series) **Wide**.

A Word of Caution

Don't keep changing your mind.

You'll annoy **KDP Select** readers if they've started reading your series in **Kindle Unlimited** and then it suddenly disappears from the subscription program.

Equally, **Wide** readers won't appreciate it if they read part way through your series, then the books disappear from the **Wide** stores because you've bundled them back into **KDP Select**.

Where you can, plant your flag and stick to it for a good long while before switching your distribution process.

Final Thoughts on Wide Versus Exclusive Distribution

The most important thing to consider when deciding whether to stay **Exclusive** or go **Wide** is it doesn't have to be all or nothing.

Take my business model for example:

- **Fiction:** I currently publish fiction **Exclusively** with **KDP Select**, because I find it hard to market and the benefits of making my novels available to **Kindle Unlimited** readers are worth it (for me).

- **Non-fiction:** I currently publish my non-fiction **Wide** to all the stores I can reach and direct through my website (I find non-fiction easier to market and I have ways of reaching more readers this way)

That's it for the **Exclusive** versus **Wide** debate!

In **Part 2**, we're going to tackle actually **Self-Publishing** your book, so buckle up.

And let's get to it.

Questions to Consider

- What are your thoughts on **Exclusive Distribution**?

- Have you weighed the pros and cons?
- If not, take some time to do that now.
- Does this sound like the right path for you?
- If so, why?
- If not, why?
- What are your thoughts on **Wide Distribution**?
- Have you weighed the pros and cons?
- If not, take some time to do that now.
- Does this sound like the right path for you?
- If so, why?
- If not, why?
- If you don't want to put all your eggs in either basket, would you consider a blended approach, with some books (or series) in **KDP Select** and some books (or series) **Wide**?
- If so, why?
- If not, why?

Part 2: Wading into the Self-Publishing Pool

Where you upload your book and smash that publish button

Self-Publishing Pillar #7

Platforms, Metadata and Hitting Publish

"There is really no reason for you not to write a book and take on this new adventure."

—Gundi Gabrielle, Kindle Bestseller Publishing

Pat yourself on the back, because you've done so much work already. You've:

- **Picked Your Publishing Path:** And pursued **Traditional Publishing** or chosen to **Independently Publish**
- **Made Your Book Camera Ready:** And sorted your cover, professional editing and formatting
- **Decided to stay Exclusive or go Wide:** And thought about which **Distribution** method is going to work for you

Doesn't it feel great to have all that prep-work done?

So, what's next?

Now it's time for the fun part, where you actually get to publish your book.

Behind Every Talented Author is a Retail Platform (or Several)

Publishing your book might seem daunting, but once you get used to it, it's actually pretty straightforward. All the major **Self-Publishing** sites are well-established and the user experience across all platforms is seamless.

Once you've filled out some required fields, uploaded your cover and manuscript files, hit publish, and waited for your book to go live on the store, people can buy (and read) your words.

I've mentioned a few of the big dog platforms in the **Self-Publishing** space already, but I'll go into a little more detail here, so you know exactly what to expect.

The Platforms

Kindle Direct Publishing (KDP)

Amazon was one of the first big companies to get into the **Self-Publishing** space. Through **KDP**, you can publish eBooks direct to the Amazon Kindle Store. You can also publish print books for customers to buy directly from Amazon.

The Kindle is the most widely used e-reader in the United States and is also popular in other English-speaking countries which have access to Amazon.

If I had to choose one platform to publish on, it would be Amazon, purely because of their market reach.

There's also the option to enroll your eBooks in Amazon's **KDP Select Program**, which we discussed in **Self-Publishing Pillar #3: Decide to Go Wide (or Stay Exclusive)**, so I won't rehash all things **Select** here.

Kobo Writing Life (KWL)

Kobo is another of the world's largest book retailers. Based out of (and hugely popular in) Canada, Kobo attracts tens of millions of readers worldwide.

Much like **Amazon KDP**, there are promotional opportunities you can only benefit from by publishing direct to Kobo.

Google Play Books

Google Play Books is an ever-growing publishing platform that caters to those of us who read on our Android devices (phones, tablets, etc.).

Again, you can access certain promotional tools by publishing to Google direct (chief among them being discount or free codes you can offer to your readers).

Provided you publish direct to the platform, you can also turn any of your published eBooks into a **Digitally Narrated Audiobook** (where one of Google Play's **Artificial Intelligence** narrator voices reads your book) for free.

A Quick Note on AI Narrated Audiobooks

The only way you can sell **Digitally Narrated Audiobooks** is by publishing them direct to Google Play Books, or selling direct from your website. The other major retailers and aggregators do **NOT** allow sales of AI narrated audio books.

As the use of AI technologies increases in the coming years, this may (and hopefully will) change, but that's how things stand at the moment.

If you are going to sell digitally narrated audio, it's a good idea to let your readers know what they're getting, because you'll disappoint them if they thought they were buying an audiobook narrated by a person, and discover it's read by a digital voice.

The easiest ways to be transparent with readers are to:

- Make it clear a digital voice narrates your book somewhere in the book's title field

- Make it clear a digital voice narrates your book somewhere in the book's product description
- Make it clear a digital voice narrates your book by getting your cover designer to add a virtual sticker to the book's cover, saying something like, "Digitally narrated".

Part of being an ethical **Self-Publisher** is being completely up front with readers about the product they're buying. If you follow these three simple steps, you can avoid grumpy readers and a series of 1-star reviews.

Aggregators

As I mentioned in the previous chapter, one drawback of publishing **Wide** is the time and effort it takes to manage your backlist across multiple platforms.

If you still want to pursue **Wide Distribution**, but don't want the hassle of managing multiple platforms, you can choose to upload your files to an **Aggregator** and they will **Distribute** your books to all the stores for you, meaning you can manage everything all in one place, through the **Aggregator's** dashboard.

NOTE: It's free to publish through an **Aggregator**, but they take a royalty-cut from each sale. Do your research before you settle on any **Aggregator**.

The Aggregators

The two main **Aggregators** in the **Self-Publishing** space are:

- **Draft2Digital (who recently acquired Smashwords):** Publishing through Draft2Digital is hands-down the easiest way to get your book into multiple stores (including Barnes and Noble, Baker & Taylor and Thalia) and library programs (like Hoopla) at once
- **Ingram Spark:** You can publish eBooks, paperbacks, and hardbacks through Ingram Spark. There's a setup fee for each book, although you can access this service for free (up to five products per month) if you're a member of *The Alliance of Independent Authors (ALLi).*

So Many Options...

With so many **Self-Publishing** options available, how in the name of paper and ink am I supposed to choose what I want to do?

That's another smart question.

I get it.

All of this can seem really overwhelming.

The choice you make will ultimately come down to how much time you have to devote to each platform.

A lot of authors start with Amazon and **KDP Select** (like I did when I published my first novel in January 2022), because it's a great way to learn the ropes without drowning in a sea of choices.

Here's how I manage my non-fiction backlist, which I publish **Wide**:

- I publish direct to Amazon, Kobo and Google Play Books because I find them easy to access direct, and I want to take advantage of the promotional opportunities you can only access by being direct with Kobo and Google Play Books
- I publish to other online retail stores and libraries using an **Aggregator,** because it's easier, and you can only access some platforms through an **Aggregator**
- I publish my non-fiction eBooks direct to my website using **Payhip** as my storefront and **PayPal** and **Stripe** to collect payments (more on **The Direct Approach** in the next chapter), because I want to benefit from the higher royalties and having a storefront I control

What Information do You Need to Self-Publish Your Book?

Now you've had a whistle-stop tour of all the major publishing platforms, let's get down to brass tacks.

What information do you need to enter on the various online stores in order to publish?

Let's look at **Metadata**!

Book Title

Shocking no-one, this is the title of your book

Book Subtitle

You don't have to use a subtitle, but it's another way you can let the reader know what they can expect from your book.

I use the subtitle: An Urban Fantasy Thriller, for my urban fantasy fiction. For my non-fiction, I used a phrase that lets the reader know what problem the book is solving. The subtitle of this book is: Self-Publishing for Authors Made Easy, for example.

The added benefit of using a subtitle is that, if readers are searching for those terms, your book is more likely to appear in search results.

Series Title

No surprises here.

If your book is part of a series, this is where you enter the series name.

Most retailers have "series pages", which link all the books in a series together (using the reading order you set).

This can be incredibly useful, because the reader usually has the option to buy the entire series at once, from the series page, resulting in higher royalties.

Series Number

This is where you specify where the book falls in your series (is it book 1, 2, 3, 4, etc.?).

Edition Number

This is more relevant for non-fiction authors, but if you decide to re-structure a book after you've written it (adding new material, cutting outdated material, re-writing large sections of the book, etc.), you'll need to publish a new edition.

If you label a book, "Second Edition", for instance, it means you've published the book a second time because you've significantly changed the original material.

Author Name

This is the penname you're publishing under.

As an example, I publish fiction under S. W. Millar and non-fiction under Shane Millar.

Contributor Names

This is where you add the names of:

- Contributing authors
- Cover designers
- Editors

Or anyone else who has helped you produce the book.

This isn't necessary, and most authors choose to give these people shout-outs in the Acknowledgements section of the book instead.

Obviously, if you co-write a book, then you would list your name, and your co-author's name, because you wrote the book together and the **Intellectual Property** belongs to both of you.

Publisher Name or Imprint Name:

If you've created a **Publishing Imprint Name**, then this is where it goes. I publish all my books under the Tagline Publishing imprint.

Product Description (or Blurb)

This is where you add the blurb that describes your book and tempts readers to buy.

Book Categories

Book categories are based on BISAC (Book Industry Standards and Communications) codes.

I know, I know, yawn-worthy... but important.

BISAC codes tell retailers, libraries, etc. which genres and sub-genres your book sits in, and where they should place them on the physical (or virtual) shelves.

For example, one category I use for my urban fantasy thriller novel, *The Witch's Revenge*, is:

Books > Mystery, Thriller & Suspense > Thrillers & Suspense > Supernatural > Witches & Wizards

And one category I use for my non-fiction books is:

Kindle Store > Kindle eBooks > Reference > Writing, Research & Publishing Guides > Genre Fiction

Whichever categories you choose, it's important to make sure you find the right fit for your book. It's no good putting a hard-boiled detective novel in a romance subcategory, because romance readers aren't looking for hard-boiled crime novels.

Pro Tip for Selecting Categories through Amazon KDP

Amazon KDP lets you select two high-level categories at the point of publishing. If you want your book to be listed in more categories (and specifically, more niche categories, to improve discoverability) you can contact **KDP Support** through your **KDP Dashboard** once you've published your book, and ask them to list it in up to 10 categories.

Need Help Finding Categories?

There are two ways I've found effective for finding more niche categories for you book:

The Free Option

If you find a book similar to yours and want to know what categories the author (or publisher if you're **Traditionally Published**) has listed it under, head over to bklnk.com (book link, without the vowels) and search the book's ASIN or ISBN number in their **Category Lookup & Book Analysis** tool.

This will bring up a list of all the book's current categories.

The Paid Option

One of my favourite publishing tools is **Publisher Rocket** from Dave Chesson over at Kindlepreneur. **Publisher Rocket** is available for a flat fee of $97.00 and comes with a 30-day money-back guarantee.

You can use **Publisher Rocket** to find **Keywords** (more on **Keywords** in a moment), categories, analyse the profit margins of books in certain categories, and search for **Amazon Ads Keywords** (more on this in the **Marketing** section).

Keywords

Amazon allows you to list seven **Keywords** (or terms people might use to search for your book) in the **Edit Book Details** section of their **Publishing Platform**, to help you improve organic discoverability.

An example of a **Keyword Phrase** I use for *The Witch's Revenge* is:

"urban fantasy orphan"

Because my main character, Henry Stone, is an orphan, and this is a common trope readers search for in the fantasy genre.

Have a think about keywords that would be relevant for your books.

ISBN

We've talked about ISBNs in a previous chapter, so I won't go over it again here.

Digital Rights Management (DRM)

You can choose to enable **Digital Rights Management**, which encrypts your book to make it harder for people to share or change your work without your permission.

The common wisdom is that enabling **DRM** is unnecessary, and it's not something I do, but do your due diligence and make your own choice.

Publication Date

Do you want to publish your book right now, or set up a **Pre-order**, so readers can order your book before publication.

Some authors use pre-orders to generate a buzz around an upcoming release, or set a long pre-order to give themselves a deadline to write the book.

The choice is yours.

NOTE: Amazon (and most of the other retailers) allow pre-orders on eBooks. Amazon does not allow pre-orders on paperbacks. Annoying I know, but if you've set a pre-order for your eBook and want to release your print book on the same day, you can set up your print book as a draft and hit publish a few days before the eBook release date.

Content

This is where you upload your high-resolution cover file (.jpeg or .png files are best for eBooks), and your manuscript (.ePub is the industry standard file type for eBooks)

What about Print Books?

If you intend to create a paperback version of your book (which I strongly suggest you consider), then you'll need all the above info (minus **DRM**, because that only applies to digital products), plus:

- **Paper Type:** White or cream (we discussed the difference between white and cream paper—and when you might want to use each type) in the **Book Covers** section

- **Trim Size:** The size your book will be (again, we spoke about this in the **Book Covers** section)

- **Bleed Settings:** The term "bleed" refers to the space between the edge of the page and the written text and, if your book has a ton of photos in it, consider enabling bleed settings to stop any funky printing issues

- **Cover Finish:** You can choose to have a glossy finish (which means your cover will be shiny) or matte (which means your cover won't be shiny). This is pure preference, but I prefer the way matte covers look, so that's what I always choose for both fiction and non-fiction.

- **Print Book Content:** Upload your cover file and manuscript (.pdf is the industry standard file-type for both print covers and manuscripts)

PREVIEWER ALERT!

BEFORE you hit publish, use the store's previewer (if they have one) to flip through both your eBook and print book to make sure everything looks like you want it to where formatting is concerned.

As great as the publishing tech we have at our fingertips is, things can go crazy, and you need to make sure your finished product looks professional.

If you want to go one step further (with your print book), you can order a **Proof Copy** before you publish. Amazon will send a physical copy of the book (with a **PROOF COPY** watermark on the cover) so you can see what the book's like "in real life" before publishing.

I did this with my first print book, because I was so nervous about screwing something up. I trust my cover designers and formatting software now, so I don't do this anymore.

Let's Talk Dollar, Dollar Bills, Y'all!

There's just one last step you need to take before you publish...

You need to set the retail price of your book.

Broadly speaking:

- eBooks cost less than print books (I price my full-length urban fantasy novels at $4.99 and my non-fiction books based on the value of the content they provide)
- Paperbacks cost less than hardbacks
- Audiobooks cost the most

Pricing is a very personal issue, because you're putting a value on the book you've poured your blood, sweat, tears, and ink into. The best advice I can give is to look at books similar to yours, see how they're priced, and go from there.

BEWARE Traditionally Published books when researching pricing. A big New York publisher might charge $9.99 for an eBook, but it's hard for **Indie-Authors** to compete with that.

Another tip is to use **Attractive Pricing**.

What do I mean by this?

It's common for books (eBook and print) to be priced at $X.99 or $X.49. These are prices readers are used to seeing and used to buying at. If you price your book at $3.22, this will look odd, and might put someone off buying it.

When you set up a print book, the retailer will give you the printing costs of the paperback or hardback. When pricing my print books, I take the printing cost and add a few dollars to ensure I'm making a profit on these.

The last thing you need to consider around pricing is international markets. Have you used **Attractive Pricing** in the US, UK, Canada, Australia, Europe, etc. Have you researched pricing in other markets like India, Japan, Mexico, etc. and worked out a reasonable price for your book in those countries.

The retailer will automatically convert international prices based on what you enter under $USD, but these prices won't be correct for that marketplace, and won't look very tempting.

Final Thoughts on Platforms, Metadata, and Hitting Publish

You're ready to hit publish!

I bet you feel pretty damn smug right now… as well you should. You've done a fantastic job to get to this point.

But what if you want to take your publishing empire to the next level?

Hold up, Shane!

Are you telling me I've got more work to do on the publishing side of things?

Well, that'll depend on whether you went **Wide** or stayed **Exclusive**, but if you really want to kick things up a notch...

You can do it with **Direct Sales**, which we're going to dive into next.

Questions to Consider

- Which platforms are you going to reach by publishing to them directly?
- Why have you made this decision?
- Which platforms are you going to reach by using an **Aggregator**?
- Why have you made this decision?
- Have you got all the information (**Metadata**) you need to publish your book on the various retail platforms?
- If not, take some time to do that now.
- Are you going to publish a print version of your book?
- If not, why not?
- Have you got all the information you need to publish your

print book on the various platforms?

- If not, take some time to do that now.
- Have you set your **Pricing**?
- Have you used **Attractive Pricing** across international marketplaces?
- Have you done your research regarding pricing in international marketplaces?
- If not, take some time to do these things now?
- Have you hit **PUBLISH!**
- If not, what the hell are you waiting for?

Self-Publishing Pillar #8

The Direct Route

"Selling direct requires a complete mindset shift. Your author store is not simply another retailer. It can be, if that's how you want to start, but an author store can be so much more."

—Morgana S. Best, Stop Making Others Rich

In the early days of **Independent Publishing**, **Direct Selling** (selling books **Direct** to readers) was notoriously difficult. This is partly because the **Indie-Publishing** infrastructure didn't support **Selling Direct** (you could do it, but it wasn't easy).

The landscape of **Direct Sales** has changed in recent years, and it's easier than ever for authors to set up an online storefront, collect payments, and distribute books to readers.

A Quick Reminder

If you choose to enroll your eBooks in to Amazon's **KDP Select** program and feature your work in **Kindle Unlimited**, you can't sell your eBooks on any other platform (including your website or storefront).

You can still sell other products (like print books) from a store you own and control using **Print on Demand (POD)** and **Drop-shipping** services.

What is Direct Selling?

Direct Selling is exactly what it sounds like.

It's when you—the author—sell your products from your website (or online storefront) to readers directly.

As with any **Publishing Path**, there are pros and cons to the **Direct Sales** approach.

Let's look at these, shall we?

The Pros of Direct Selling

If you approach publishing from an e-commerce point of view, and think of yourself as a store owner (rather than an **Independent Author**) there are lots of pros to **Direct Selling**:

- **Money: Direct Sales** is the best way to keep the highest percentage of royalties from any sales you make. **Independent Authors** who only publish through the retail stores keep between 35% and 75% of royalties. Authors who sell **Direct** keep over 90% of their royalties.

- **Payment:** When a customer pays for a book on your site, you receive payment within 24-48 hours. Any payments you receive from the other stores take around 60 days to reach you.

- **Data:** When you **Sell Direct** and link your store to your **Mailing List** (more on **Mailing Lists** in the **Marketing** section) you can capture customer details and transfer them straight to your mailing list so you can keep in touch with them (something you can't do with the online stores)

- **Discount Codes:** You can offer discount codes to readers and put your books "on sale" without having to alter prices on all the other stores

- **Visibility:** When you send readers to the online retail stores, they fill your book page with other author's books related to yours (an example of this includes the "**Also Boughts**" carousel on Amazon). On your store, the only products readers can see are yours, so you minimize the risk of them clicking away from your books.

- **In-Store Exclusives:** Say you're publishing a box set, and you want to price it at $14.99. If you publish through Amazon, the royalty rate would be 35% per sale (because it's priced over $9.99). Selling the same product direct through your site means you keep over 90% of royalties.

- **Early Releases:** This is a strategy that's worked with my non-fiction. I usually put the book up for pre-order on all the major stores then—a week before release—I'll make the book available direct through my **Payhip** store, and advertise on social media and in (appropriate) writer's groups. This way, I can generate almost instant income, while also building pre-orders on the major stores.

The Cons of Direct Selling

If you think I sound gah-gah about **Direct Sales**, let's provide some balance (so you've got all the facts). The cons of direct selling are:

- **Time:** Depending on the size of your backlist, setting up your store takes a bit of time.

- **Visibility:** Visibility is a double-edged sword where **Direct Selling** is concerned. It's hard enough to drive traffic to the major book retailers, and even harder to drive traffic to your own store. If you have a reader-base already (or you can promote in other ways, e.g., if you have a podcast with enough listeners, or YouTube channel with enough subscribers) it'll be easier to get the word out.

- **Set-up costs:** You'll need to distribute your books (eBook and print), which has set-up costs (more on this later) and a storefront (there are free and paid options for this, depending on the store features you need, and whether you want to sell print direct)

- **Backend Admin:** If you want to maximise your store, it's a good idea to set up automated email sequences based on the products your readers buy (this way, you can cross sell and/or upsell related items)
- **More Work:** I'm not suggesting you completely forego the major retailers, and recommend **Publishing Wide** in tandem with **Selling Direct**. This means your store is another platform you need to upload everything to and manage.

What You'll Need to Sell Direct

So, based on the pros and cons of **Direct Sales**, do you think it could work for you?

If so, here are the basic things you'll need to get started.

A Storefront

As mentioned above, there are free and paid options for storefronts. If you only want to sell eBooks and digital products, a free storefront could work best for you. If you want to sell print books as well, then you'll need to look at a paid option.

FREE

A great option for setting up a free storefront is Payhip, which is the platform I currently use for **Direct Sales**. Payhip is user friendly, and gives you the opportunity to sell eBooks, Audiobooks, and online courses **Direct**.

Another tremendous benefit to using Payhip is they handle **EU VAT** on any sales you make in an **EU Territory**.

PAID

One of the best paid options for setting up your storefront is Shopify, which is the platform I'll be using when I'm able to sell print books direct.

The **Basic Shopify Plan** costs $29.00 per month, and gives you everything you need to build an e-commerce author business selling direct to customers.

You get:

- An online storefront (which you can customize to your liking)
- The ability to add as many products as you want
- The option to link your store to your social media accounts, so readers can buy books through the social platforms without clicking away
- The ability to integrate your store with a paperback **Print on Demand (POD)** service (which means you don't have to store print books at a physical location)

- Integration with your mailing list
- And more...

A Distribution Method

Simply put, you need to get your books to your readers.

EBOOKS

The best way to deliver eBooks to readers is Book Funnel.

I say this because they handle all the customer support. If someone doesn't know how to side-load a book onto their e-reader, you can direct them to the Book Funnel customer support team, and they'll handle everything for you.

How cool is that?

It's a lifesaver, I promise you!

In order to sell books direct, you'll need a paid Book Funnel account. The **First-Time Author Plan** costs $20.00 per year, and gives you everything you need to distribute eBooks.

PRINT BOOKS

There are two well-known options for setting up **Print On Demand (POD)** for your online store.

The first is Lulu Xpress. There aren't any set-up costs to **Self-Publish** through them, but they will charge you the manufacturing, shipping, and fulfillment costs when a customer places an order.

The second option is Book Vault. It costs £19.95 to add a title to their database. It's free to upload new cover and manuscript files, and you'll need to pay the printing and dispatch costs when a customer places an order. Some authors choose to use Book Vault because they have a wider range of **Trim Sizes** than Lulu Xpress.

A Way to Collect Payment

There are tons of options for collecting payment from customers.

Some of the well-known ones include:

- **PayPal:** If you choose PayPal, it's best to set up a PayPal Business account and request to apply micro-payments. This means you'll pay lower transaction fees and keep more royalties, because books are lower priced products.
- **Stripe:** The perfect way to collect card payments easily.
- **Shopify Payments:** If you choose Shopify as your storefront, you can enable **Shopify Payments** (there aren't any transaction fees with this method).

Connecting your various payment-taking methods to your storefront of choice is relatively easy, and the store you use will have clear, step-by-step instructions on how to do this.

The Same Things You Need on the Major Retailers

You still need:

- Book Cover files
- Manuscript files
- Book descriptions (Blurbs)
- Book Metadata
- Etc.

Hold the Phone!

Hold the phone, Shane! This all sounds...

Daunting.

Trust me. I get it.

When I first dove into the deep end of the **Direct Sales** pool, I was overwhelmed, too. But remember, you don't have to do everything all at once. I set up my Payhip store slowly, adding one product at a time, making sure the integration with Book Funnel and my mailing list worked, and making sure I could collect payments without hassle.

I also spent a good chunk of time watching a ton of YouTube tutorials on how to get everything right.

Don't rush this... or—if you feel like it's not for you right now—come back to it when you can devote the bandwidth to it.

There is a Silver Lining...

Believe me when I tell you, I'm not what you would call "techie".

I had no experience with e-commerce and direct selling prior to May 2022. If I can do it, you can, too!

It just takes patience, persistence, and a little trial and error.

Final Thoughts on the Direct Route

Can you see how **Direct Sales** gives you the opportunity to make more money with your writing, forge stronger relationships with readers, and give you more creative control?

If this sounds good to you, then **Selling Direct** (although overwhelming at first glance) might be the route for you!

That's your lot for **Part 2: Wading into the Self-Publishing Pool**.

Next up we're looking at the bane of every **Independent Author's** existence... **Marketing and Promotion**... only joking (sort of).

Questions to Consider

- What attracts you to **Direct Sales**?
- What makes you run for the hills when you hear the words **Direct Sales**?
- If you want to try **Direct Selling**, which storefront will you choose, and why?
- Have you checked out Book Funnel for **Distribution**?
- If not, take some time to do that now.
- Do you want to sell print books **Direct**?
- If so, have you checked out Lulu Xpress or Book Vault for **Distribution**?
- If not, take some time to do that now.
- How will you collect payments from customers who buy your books?

Part 3: Post-Publishing

Where we look at some tips and tricks you can use to market your book

Self-Publishing Pillar #9

The Call to Action

"A call to action, typically abbreviated as CTA, is simply a request for your reader to do something."
—Sean Platt, Johnny B. Truant, and David Wright, Write. Publish. Repeat.

I MADE A BIG mistake when I first got into writing.

Huge, actually.

I thought I knew how to write a novel (**SPOILER ALERT:** I didn't). This means I spent all my time (outside of writing) learning about the author business, marketing, and promotion.

I knew about:

- Building an author brand *before* I was an author

- The ins and outs of paid advertising *before* I had any books to advertise
- Several marketing strategies *before* I had any books to market

At this very early stage of my career, I should have been learning how to write.

That's why I held off on publishing a book on the mechanics of successful **Self-Publishing** until *after* I'd written a collection of books on the writing craft.

Because it's the order I wish I'd learned everything in.

Imagine how frustrating it is knowing how to make money as an author, and having nothing to sell.

With that, I hope you have at least one book to market at this point.

If not, and you're like me, you're going to want to know all the marketing stuff anyway, and nothing I say is going to stop you from learning.

So, let's do this thing!

Let Me Ask You a Question?

When is the best time to market to readers?

That's right!

It's when they finish your book.

Think about this. Your reader has just made it to the end of your novel. They've spent hundreds of pages with your plot, your characters, and your settings. If you've done your job right, they're hooked, and they loved your book.

They're primed to want to help you out.

How can you best take advantage of this (ethically)?

The Call to Action

If you've not heard the term before, a **Call to Action (CTA)** is an instruction you give the reader to get them to take an action. This action could be to buy your next book, to sign up to your mailing list, or to leave a review on the retailer where they bought the book.

Where Should You Put the CTA?

There are lots of different opinions about where CTAs should go, and I've experimented with a few of them. What's always worked best for me is including the CTA as soon as the book ends.

You've typed the last sentence of your book.

Leave a space, or insert an ornamental break, and right underneath—on the same page—include your CTA.

CAUTION!

I recommend including only one or two CTAs at the back of your book.

Why?

Because the more actions you ask your readers to take, the less likely they are to do any of them.

Five CTAs You Can Start With

The Purchase CTA

Do you write in a series? If so, is the next book available for pre-order or purchase? This is the perfect place to ask your reader to pre-order or buy your next book.

In fact, many **Independently Published** authors throw up a long pre-order just so they can include this CTA at the back of their book. This is anecdotal, but authors who use this approach have reported greater read-through from Book 1 to Book 2, Book 3 to Book 4, and so on.

An example of **The Purchase CTA**:

Thanks for reading The Witch's Revenge, and joining Henry on his quest for justice. Want to know what happens next? Buy Book 2, The Coven's Executioner, NOW!
[Link to product page for Book 2]

PRO TIP

Use a site like *Books2Read* to create a **Universal Book Link (UBL)**.

What in the name of all things bookish is a **Universal Book Link**?

Another stellar question!

It's a shortened link that takes your reader to a landing page which shows them everywhere your book is on sale. Better still, when they click on their preferred store, the **UBL** takes them to that store in their country.

This means if a customer in New York clicks to buy from the Amazon store, they go to the amazon.com page for your book, whereas it would take someone clicking in London to the amazon.co.uk page.

Want to know the best thing about Books2Read?

It's free!

The Mailing List CTA

Have you set up a mailing list readers can sign up to for regular writerly updates, new release notifications, special offers, and a way to communicate with you?

If not, then what are you waiting for (more on mailing lists—and their crucial importance—in the next chapter)?

The end of your book is the perfect place to ask readers to sign up to your mailing list, especially if you're giving away a reader magnet (a prequel short story, novella in your series, a deleted scene from your book, etc.) in exchange for their email address.

Here's an example of a **Mailing List CTA**:

Thanks for reading The Witch's Revenge and joining Henry on his quest for justice. Want more from the Myth & Magic universe? You can download your FREE copy of The Thief's Magic and find out how Geek got to COVEN NOW!
[Link to mailing list signup page]

The Review CTA

One of the simplest ways to get organic reviews on your books is to ask for them at the end of your novel.

Here's an example of a **Review CTA**:

Thanks for reading The Witch's Revenge and joining Henry on his quest for justice. If you enjoyed the story, and have a moment to spare, I'd appreciate a short, honest review on the store where you bought the book. Reviews are so important for authors because they help

new readers, like you, discover our work.
[Links to the various retailers review pages]

The Upsell CTA

Do you write fiction, and have physical merchandise (bookmarks, mugs, t-shirts, hoodies, etc.) related to your series. You could include a CTA directing people to buy something from your merch store.

Here's an example you could use:

Thanks for reading The Witch's Revenge and joining Henry on his quest for justice. Want to grab your own COVEN Trainee T-shirt TODAY? Visit my store and use coupon code ***IHEARTCOVEN*** *at checkout for 50% off.*
[Link to product page on your store]

What if, like me, you write non-fiction for writers and also offer developmental editing services?

You could include a CTA similar to this:

Thanks for reading How to Edit Your Novel: Self-Revisions for Authors Made Easy. Need a developmental editor? You can check out my Write Better Fiction Editing Services NOW!
[Link to Editing Services page]

The Social Media CTA

Looking to grow your social media following, and attract readers to your various pages? You can ask fans to follow you, like this:

> *Thank you for reading The Witch's Revenge and joining Henry on his quest for justice. I love hearing from readers, and it would be great to connect. You can follow me on social media NOW!*
> *[Links to social media profiles]*

This list is not exhaustive. Get creative with your CTAs and think about what reader action would benefit you most right now. The sky really is the limit with CTAs.

But, Shane... Which CTA Should I Use?

Hang on, though! I want my readers to do all those things. If I should only include one or two CTAs at the back of my book, which one should I use?

Yet again, fantastic questioning skills, Columbo!

Here's my answer:

Use the CTA you need the most

What do you need right now?

Want more sales on Book 2? Consider going with the **Purchase CTA**. Little or no reviews on your book? Perhaps it would be best to use the **Review CTA**. Light on mailing list subscribers? Maybe it's time to break out the **Mailing List CTA**?

When I published my first novel in January 2022, my major focus was getting reviews, because I only had one book, and I wanted the social proof reviews provide ready for when Book 2 came out.

So, I included a **Review CTA** at the back.

My focus has shifted to read-through recently, so I've changed my fiction **CTA** to a **Purchase CTA**.

And remember, I said you could include one or two **CTAs**.

My second CTA is always a **Mailing List** CTA, because I know how important being able to reach readers using email is.

Focus on what you need right now, and you won't go wrong with **CTAs**.

Final Thoughts on Calls to Action

Can you see how this simple strategy can aid your marketing efforts and make it easier to bring readers into your author ecosystem?

Great!

In that case—

Wait!

Everything... okay?

I get the whole CTA thing, really. But that only helps me market to existing readers... so how the hell do I get people to read my books in the first place?

Excellent point!

Good thing I've dedicated the rest of **Part 3: Post-Publishing** to marketing and advertising strategies and tactics you can use to attract new readers.

Over the coming chapters, we'll be delving into:

- The power of an author website and mailing list
- Content marketing
- Social media marketing
- Paid advertising
- Newsletter swaps

Excited? You look it. You should be.

Let's dive in!

Questions to Consider

- Have you included a **Call to Action (CTA)** in the back of your book?
- If not, when are you going to include one?
- Which type of CTA are you going to use?
- Would a **Purchase CTA** serve you best right now?
- Would a **Mailing List CTA** serve you best right now?
- Would a **Review CTA** serve you best right now?
- Would an **Upsell CTA** serve you best right now?
- Would a **Social Media CTA** serve you best right now?
- Come up with a list of creative **CTAs** you can use to promote other aspects of your work.

Self-Publishing Pillar #10

Your Website and Mailing List

"While I have a much bigger Twitter following and a thriving Facebook Page, along with one of the most popular blogs in the industry, my mailing list is much more important than all of those things combined."
—David Gaughran, Following

Why do I need a website and mailing list if I want to market my books?

It's a valid question with a simple answer.

Owning your own website gives you a place to send readers where they can find out more about you, your books, and everything you do online. Plus, they won't see tons of unrelated content (like they do on the retail stores). Owning your own mailing list means you can stay in touch with readers, send them updates, new releases, special offers, freebies... the list is endless.

But...

Do I really need a website and a mailing list...? It sounds like a lot of work.

It is a lot of work, but I promise you it's worth it.

Lower the raised eyebrow and I'll explain why.

Owning Your Own Space on the Internet is Important Because...

Say a reader buys your book from Amazon, reads all the way to the end, and wants to know more about you and your books. Yes, you could send them to one of your social media profiles with a well-placed **CTA**... but you don't own that space.

Let me ask you a few questions:

- What if your account gets suspended for reasons beyond your control?
- What if the platform in question changes their algorithm (which they frequently do), which means your posts aren't getting seen?

- What if your platform of choice loses popularity, or disappears completely, and takes your entire following with it (Myspace, anyone)?

When you build your house on someone else's land, you're renting. The all-powerful Facebook, Twitter, Instagram, TikTok, or ____________ [INSERT SOCIAL MEDIA PLATFORM OF CHOICE HERE] landlords can evict you.

And there's diddly squat you can do about it.

But...

When you build your house on land you own, it's yours, and no-one can take it away from you.

That's what you're doing when you have a website and a mailing list.

Building on land you own.

Not all Websites Were Created Equal

You can build a website for free, or pay for hosting. If you decide to use a free package to create your author base-of-operations, you don't own it.

The platform you've built it on can still shut you down and turf you out onto the street.

It's best to pay for **Web Hosting**.

This means you pay a company to host all the data for your website on one of their servers (basically, they store all the information on your website in their virtual lock-up).

When you pay for hosting, you own your website, and the only person who can shut it down is you.

Now there's a powerful thought!

When you're first starting out (and your website doesn't get much traffic), hosting doesn't have to cost you the earth. Plenty of hosting companies (like Bluehost, the one I currently use) offer cheaper hosting plans for beginners.

What happens when my website gets more traffic?

You can either upgrade your plan with your current hosting provider, or switch to a different hosting provider based on your needs.

That's the beauty of owning your own space.

But, I'm not a web designer, Shane.

Yeah, me neither. Far from it.

The good news is, you don't have to be.

If you use a company like WordPress, Squarespace, or Wix, you can design your website in a few simple clicks using free or paid **Themes** (design templates) and **Plugins** (apps).

Designing a website has never been easier.

What is a Mailing List?

So, what exactly is a mailing list?

A mailing list lets you email anyone who has subscribed to your newsletter, so you can send them:

- Updates about your writing life
- Updates about your personal life (this doesn't mean you have to share everything, you can be selective, and some people don't share any details about their personal life)
- New releases
- Special offers and sales
- Cover reveals
- Snippets from the novel you're currently working on
- And anything else you think your readers might be interested in...

Why Bother?

I already have to write my books, get brilliant covers, get a **Professional Edit**, Format, include CTAs, and upload my books...

Do I really need to bother with a **Mailing List**?

The short answer is yes.

Think of all your favourite brands and companies:

- How many of them do you get emails from?
- How often do you take an action based on those emails?
- How often do you buy from them based on the emails you receive?

Why do you think all the best companies take this approach to email marketing?

Because they know all about the power of a **Mailing List**.

They understand the value of **Know, Like, and Trust**.

The more your readers get to **Know** you through regular email communication, the more they will **Like** you (providing your giving them content they enjoy), and the more they will **Trust** you.

And readers buy books from people they trust.

You can never build that level of trust with a customer who only has contact with you through one of the major retailers, because the major retailers will **NEVER** give you access to their customer's email addresses.

Why You Need a Sweetener

No, I'm not talking about adding sugar to your morning cup of coffee to put an extra pep in your step.

The sweetener I'm referring to is a **Reader Magnet**.

What in the name of Stephen King's ever-loving back-catalogue is a **Reader Magnet**?

A **Reader Magnet** is a digital product you offer readers (for free) in exchange for their email address and a spot on your coveted mailing list. It would be great if readers wanted to sign up to your mailing list in droves without an incentive, but that's not how the world works.

Hold on!

So, you're telling me I have to create something, then give it away for free for no financial gain?

No.

One, it depends on your author goals. If you want to make money doing this, then having a mailing list is key. Two, I'm saying you should create something, then give it away in exchange for the reader's email address.

Remember... **Know, Like, and Trust** equals more sales over the long run, because those customers are more likely to be repeat buyers.

Don't underestimate the power of being able to contact your readers directly any time you need to.

It's a game changer.

And, some reader magnets don't take a great deal of time investment. For example:

- The sweetener I use for my fiction list is a prequel short story in my *Myth & Magic* series, which features an adventure told from the point of view of a popular side character from the first book.

- The sweetener I use for my non-fiction list is a PDF Cheat Sheet, which provides a quick and dirty overview of the **Write Better Fiction Key Beats**, which is the outlining system I talk about in my book *How to Plot Your Novel*

Both these things were (relatively) quick to create, and go a long way to incentivizing readers to sign up for my list.

There are tons of things you could offer as a reader magnet:

- Character dossiers

- Fantasy maps (if you're a fantasy author)

- Self-narrated audio short stories

- Deleted scenes

- A sneak peek from the next book in your series

- An extended epilogue

Remember Book Funnel?

You can use it to deliver your **Reader Magnet**.

It's beyond this book to discuss mailing lists in great depth. If you're looking for a fantastic resource on this topic, I highly recommend *Newsletter Ninja* and *Newsletter Ninja 2* by Tammi Labrecque.

Final Thoughts on Your Website and Mailing List

The important thing to consider when deciding what you want to do about your website and mailing list is:

Do you want to build your author hub on rented land, or land you own?

Think about your author goals and take a long-term view. What could your author business become, and what would it mean to have unlimited contact with your readers, and somewhere to send them when they want more?

Questions to Consider

- What steps can you take right now to build your author website?
- What steps can you take right now to build your mailing list?
- What type of reader magnet are you going to offer potential

mailing list subscribers?

- What steps can you take right now to create your **Reader Magnet**?

Self-Publishing Pillar #11

Content Marketing

"Content marketing is creating and sharing online material like articles, audio, video, and images that don't explicitly market products but instead attract attention to your website or profile."
—Joanna Penn, How to Market a Book

I wanted to touch on **Content Marketing** because it's a great way to market your books for free.

Well...

Not completely free, it costs you your time, but if you're light on funds, it's a sensible approach to **Marketing**.

What is Content Marketing?

When authors do **Content Marketing**, they produce:

- Blog posts
- Articles
- YouTube Videos
- Social media content
- Podcast interviews
- And more...

Related to their books.

You could make the argument that it's easier for non-fiction authors to leverage **Content Marketing** and make it successful and, to some extent that's true. It's easier to find opportunities to create free content for non-fiction that markets your books.

Take the non-fiction side of my business, for instance. I produce regular articles for the Fictionary blog, which contain links to my non-fiction books, author website, and developmental editing services. I've also appeared on multiple podcasts for writers, talking about the subjects of my writing guides.

It's also easier for non-fiction authors (particularly writers who write about anything related to being an author) to start their own podcast for authors, which helps with book promotion.

Examples of writing podcasts include:

- The Creative Penn Podcast
- The Rebel Author Podcast
- The Next Level Authors Podcast
- The Sell More Books Show
- The Dialogue Doctor Podcast

What About Fiction Authors?

While more challenging, fiction authors can still make **Content Marketing** successful.

You can:

- Appear on podcasts for fiction fans (in your niche)
- Create a fiction podcast, where you read your books
- Use social media, or your blog, to share a behind-the-scenes look at your writing life (where you write, your research process, etc.)
- Write articles based around the common themes in your fiction and post them to your blog (or sell them to a third-party blogging site)

Get Creative

Much like many of the marketing tactics and strategies I'm sharing, the more creative you can be the better.

Final Thoughts on Content Marketing

Marketing doesn't have to cost you the earth, and there are plenty of things you can do for free that will help spread the word about your books.

If you're willing to put in the time, **Content Marketing** can be an effective way to bring readers into your author ecosystem.

Questions to Consider

- Spend five to ten minutes listing every single **Content Marketing** idea you can think of.
- Which of these do you think will work best?
- What steps can you take to produce things you can use in your **Content Marketing**?

Self-Publishing Pillar #12

Social Media Marketing

"To generate such a buzz for such a low cost is very difficult with any other marketing channel [said in reference to social media]."

—Tim Cameron-Kitchen and Yvonne Ivanescu, Profitable Social Media Marketing

Hold your horses there, Shane! Isn't **Social Media Marketing** part of my **Content Marketing Strategy**. Didn't we just talk about that?

You're right.

Social Media Marketing is **Content Marketing**, but it's also its own unique thing, so it deserves its own section.

Social Media is Not a Market Stall

A lot of newer authors make a huge mistake where social media is concerned. They treat it like a market stall, and it's not. While shouting, "Get ya plums, a pound a punnet!" works really well for the market trader who owns a fruit and veg stall, it doesn't work for books.

Posting "Buy my book, it's really awesome!" is a surefire way to turn readers off.

Am I saying you can never promote your books on social media, or never drop a **Call to Action** to drive sales?

No.

But I am saying you should do this sparingly.

Opinions on how often you should promote your books on social media vary, but most authors agree that only 10%-20% of your posts should be of the, "Buy my book!" variety.

Say what? So, what the hell am I supposed to post about the other 80%-90% of the time?

Don't worry... I've got you covered.

How to Make the Most of Social Media Marketing

So, if you can't constantly blitz readers with promotional messages, what can you do?

You need to create **Content Buckets** (and group your posts together) based on what you want to achieve?

The Four Social Media Content Buckets

There are four main **Content Buckets** you can draw from when planning out your social media posts:

Bucket #1: The Social Bucket

So many people forget the "social" in **Social Media**. Not only should you like, share, and comment on other people's posts, you should also create posts that drive a sense of community and spark conversation.

Examples of **Social Posts** authors can use are:

- **This or That Posts:** Do you write fantasy? Ask your followers whether they prefer dragons or magicians and why. Thrillers? James Bond or Lara Croft? These fun posts can spark a lot of conversation and foster a sense of belonging.
- **Currently Reading Posts:** Read any good books lately? Post about a book you enjoyed and ask your followers what they're reading right now. Again, it's a great way to start a conversation. Readers (and authors) love to talk about books.
- **Netflix and Chill Post:** Similar to a **Currently Reading**

Post, but related to what you're watching right now.

The sole purpose of **The Social Bucket** is to build a connection between you and your followers.

But...

Please be genuine!

More than anything, **The Social Bucket** is about building *genuine* connections with your followers. Don't use this content bucket to manipulate your followers into liking you.

Treat it like you're chatting to your friends, and readers will love you for it.

Bucket #2: The Behind the Curtain Bucket

Readers want to see behind the curtain.

They want to know:

- Where you write
- What your writing process looks like
- How much progress you've made on an upcoming book
- What your hobbies are
- How you spend your spare time

- Whether you've taken any interesting trips
- Tidbits from your personal life (only the things you're comfortable sharing, of course)

Readers want to get to know you. I don't mean the "super-shiny-public-persona" you. They want to know the everyday you.

So, give them a little of that, in a way that doesn't make you feel uncomfortable.

Some of my most popular posts are photos of the mugs I drink from, or interesting meals I'm eating (I'll emphasize the word "interesting" here, because no-one wants to see the Corn Flakes I'm eating for breakfast), or the odd photo I post of my particularly crazy bed hair.

Be a real person... because you are one!

Bucket #3: The Inspiration Bucket

Readers love to be inspired, so inspire them.

Tell them:

- Why you write
- What sparked the idea for your latest work in progress?
- About any life-changing inspirational quotes you've heard recently, discuss what they mean to you, and ask for follower's opinions
- About any inspirational experiences you've had recently

Bucket #4: The Education Bucket

I'll admit, this is easier for non-fiction authors who write in the "how to" or "self-help" space, because you always have something to teach.

You can share:

- Your top tips on knitting (or whatever your area of expertise is)
- Lessons learned from discovering how to ____________ [area of expertise]
- A targeted post teaching a specific piece of knowledge

But...

Fiction authors can teach, too.

You could talk about:

- How your genre came to be
- Interesting facts you learned when researching your latest novel
- The history behind your fictional world (educating the reader about your fictional universe)

Final Thoughts on Social Media Marketing

See?

You don't have to ram your books down people's throats every time you post (which is a good thing, because books would be hard—and painful—to swallow). There are plenty of things you can entice your readers with without coming across like a door-to-door vacuum cleaner salesman from the 1970s.

Questions to Consider

- What kinds of content can fill your **Social Bucket**?
- What kinds of content can fill your **Behind the Curtain Bucket**?
- What kinds of content can fill your **Inspiration Bucket**?
- What kinds of content can fill your **Education Bucket**?

Self-Publishing Pillar #13

Paid Advertising

"Paid advertising is difficult, but many feel it is necessary to sell books. You should consider this with caution because it is easy to lose a significant amount of money if you do not know what you are doing on the advertising platforms."

—J. Thorn, How to Self-Publish

Ah, paid advertising.

The big, bad boogeyman that strikes fear into the hearts of authors everywhere.

And I get it... I really do.

Taking part in any form of paid advertising means spending money to promote your book with no guarantees of a return.

It's scary, but it's necessary... eventually.

There's a prevailing wisdom in the **Indie-Author** community that we operate in a "pay-to-play" market, meaning that we need to spend money to promote our books, otherwise no-one will ever discover them.

My view isn't quite that bleak.

I really believe in the power of **Content Marketing**, when it's done properly and ethically, and it drives a steady flow of sales.

But...

Paying to show your book to potential readers is unavoidable if you want to sell books at scale.

Why?

Because you can target the right readers and get their eyes on your book much quicker than you can with **Content Marketing**.

If you really don't have the budget to invest in paid advertising, then double down on **Content Marketing**. You can still be successful as an author using this approach. Just know it will take you longer.

If you have a budget for paid advertising, then buckle up buttercup, because we're going down the **Paid Advertising** rabbit-hole...

When Should I Start with Paid Advertising?

The answer will frustrate you.

It depends.

Here are some things to consider about paid advertising before you dive in:

- **It can be costly:** You need to make sure you can afford it
- **It works better when you have a bigger backlist:** It's more profitable to advertise Book 1 in a series when there's a good chance readers will buy Books 2, 3, 4, and 5 in the series.
- **There's a learning curve:** Do you understand the difference between **Cost-Per-Click (CPC)** and **Average Cost Per Sale (ACOS)**? Do you know your **Bidding Strategy**? Do you know how to work out your **Conversion Rate**?

What Types of Paid Advertising Can I Do?

It's beyond this book to go into **Paid Advertising** in extensive depth. I'll give you the broad strokes here.

There are three major types of **Paid Advertising** we **Indie-Authors** can take advantage of:

- **Newsletter List Services**
- **Cost-Per-Click (CPC) Advertising**

- **Newsletter Swaps**

Let's look at each of these, so you know what to expect.

Newsletter List Services

When you use a **Newsletter List Service**, you pay them a flat fee to advertise your book on their genre-specific newsletters. These services cater largely to free and discounted books, so they work great when you're running a $0.99 sale or free promotion.

They also work well for advertising **Permafree** books.

Running promotions like this can be extremely powerful because these newsletters are curated, and their subscribers are:

- Readers
- Highly targeted
- Used to purchasing books through them

A popular strategy when using **Newsletter List Services** is to use a technique called **Ad-Stacking**. This means you book a series of promotions with the various **List Services** over a period of several days, starting with the smaller lists and building to the larger ones.

Ad-Stacking is popular because, on algorithmically driven online retailers (like Amazon), your books will stay on the bestseller lists longer if you sales build slowly over time, as opposed to spiking one day, then disappearing the next.

Examples of **Newsletter List Services** include:

- Freebooksy
- Bargainbooksy
- Robin Reads
- E-reader News Today (ENT)
- Book Barbarian (primarily for fantasy)

Each review site has its own specifications, which determine whether they'll accept your book for a promotion (e.g., many—but not all—specify that you need a certain number of reviews to be considered).

A Note on BookBub Featured Deals

If you're lucky enough to get a **BookBub Featured Deal**, this is arguably the most powerful form of **Newsletter List Service Promotion**. While **BookBub** have accepted books enrolled in **KDP Select (Exclusive)** in the past, they're far more likely to accept **Wide** books.

BookBub Featured Deals are in high demand. Securing a slot on this newsletter can be difficult. You may have to apply a bunch of times before you get accepted.

Cost-Per-Click Advertising

Newsletter List Services aren't the only way to promote your books.

You can also run **Cost-Per-Click Ads** on Facebook, Amazon, BookBub (which differs from the **BookBub Featured Deal**), and a bunch of other places.

Here's an overview of how **Cost-Per-Click Advertising** works:

- **Step #1—Targeting:** You target potential customers using keywords, book titles, author names, and anything else that could lead to sales (the trick is to target potential customers based on other books and search terms that are like yours)

- **Step #2—Daily Budget:** You set a maximum daily budget that the **Advertising Platform** can't exceed (e.g., if you set your daily budget at $5.00 per day, you will only spend a maximum of $5.00 per day)

- **Step #3—Bidding:** You choose how much you'd like to bid (spend) to secure an advert (e.g., if you choose to bid $0.39 per click, you will pay $0.39—or somewhere near $0.39, depending on your **Bidding Strategy**) every time someone clicks on your ad

- **Step #4—Impressions:** Once you've launched your ad, it will generate **Impressions**, which is the term used when the advertising platform shows your ad (if the platform shows your ad 1,000 times, then that ad has generated 1,000 impressions)

- **Step #5—Clicks:** You only pay if someone clicks your ad (**Impressions** are free)
- **Step #6—Orders:** One order is one sale
- **Step #7—Conversion Rate:** Shows how well your ad is converting (fewer **Clicks** + higher **Orders** = more sales = better **Conversion Rate**)
- **Step #8:** Rinse and repeat

Cost-Per Click Advertising can be an extremely effective way to sell books, if you know what you're doing and source enough **Relevant Keywords**.

The word **Relevancy** is key.

If you write thrillers, it's no good advertising based on romance keywords.

Similarly, targeting high-profile authors in your genre can be costly. If you can niche down and target so-called "lesser known" authors, this tactic can prove lucrative.

Newsletter Swaps

The last major way to advertise your books is to take part in **Newsletter Swaps**. A **Newsletter Swap** is when you agree to promote a book (or books) written by another author in your genre to your newsletter list if they agree to promote one of your books.

You can either arrange this privately if you know a lot of authors in your genre (in which case, it would be free), or you can use a paid service (like Book Funnel or StoryOrigin) to enter a **Newsletter Swap**.

As with all advertising, be specific.

Don't promote your friend's hard-boiled crime thriller to your fantasy list or vice versa.

That'll just lead to reader confusion and disappointment (and potentially a ton of unsubscribes).

And that's the last thing any of us wants or needs.

Want to Know More About Paid Advertising?

If you want to know more about paid advertising, and get into it on a much deeper level, I highly recommend the following resources:

- *Self-Publishing with Amazon Ads* by Bryan Cohen
- *BookBub Ads Expert* by David Gaughran
- *Amazon Ads for Indie Authors* by Janet Margot
- Mark Dawson's *Ads for Authors* online course (premium product)

- Bryan Cohen's *Author Ad School* (premium product)

Final Thoughts on Paid Advertising

The saying goes you have to spend money to make money.

It's true.

If your goal is to make money from your books, prepare to invest in paid advertising at some point (if not now, then later, when your **Content Marketing** efforts pay off and you make a profit).

But...

Effective **Paid Advertising** can really scale your sales.

Questions to Consider

- Would **paid advertising** work for you financially?
- If not, how can you ramp up your **Content Marketing** efforts to make some money to invest in **Paid Advertising**?
- If so, how much money can you set aside each month to invest in **Paid Advertising**?

- Have you researched **Newsletter List Services**?
- Which ones are you going to try?
- Have you considered **Ad Stacking**?
- What are you going to do about **Cost-Per-Click Advertising**?
- What do you need to learn to delve into **Cost-Per-Click Advertising**?
- Have you arranged any **Newsletter Swaps** (either privately, or using a paid service like Book Funnel or StoryOrigin)?
- If not, what steps do you need to take to facilitate **Newsletter Swaps**?

Conclusion

And That's A Wrap... For Now

You did it!

I'm proud of you, my writerly friend.

You've put in a lot of work, and now you know exactly what you need to do to **Self-Publish** a book (and the basics of book **Marketing**).

I know how nerve-wracking smashing that **PUBLISH** button is. So, if you haven't given your book the green light yet, I get it.

You're scared.

It scared me, too.

If you're feeling overwhelmed and/or you haven't answered the questions at the end of each chapter yet, take some time to do that now.

Then hit publish!

I promise, the more books you publish, the easier it gets. And, who knows, you might even catch the author bug.

If you're still hesitant, think about what publishing books could mean for your future. More money? Connections in the writing community... maybe even a gateway out of your day job, if that's what you're looking for.

The world is your oyster.

The sky's the limit.

[Insert your favourite motivational cliché here].

You can do this thing!

I believe in you, and wish you every success on your **Self-Publishing** path.

Happy writing.

Cheers

Shane

Grab Your FREE Write Better Fiction Key Beats Cheat Sheet TODAY!

Want to Discover the Nine Key Beats Every Novel Needs?

Grab your FREE copy of *The Write Better Fiction Key Beats Cheat Sheet* NOW!

Visit: https://bit.ly/writebetterfictionbeats

Acknowledgments

First, foremost, and always, thank you to my family and friends for your unwavering encouragement and support. You keep me grounded, and I couldn't do this without you.

Special shout out to Joanna Penn. If I hadn't Googled *How to Market a Book* on New Year's Day 2019, I never would've gotten started as an independent author, or been so motivated to give this thing a real shot.

To my long time ARC readers, who read most of the books (if not every single book) I write: Sassy Cassie Newell, Matt Goodall, Sarah Louise, The Mysterious Maggie M, Scott Williamson, and Herman Steuernagel. You folks rock!

Thank you to the authors who've mentored me, I couldn't be more grateful. You know who you are. I owe you more than I can say.

To all the writers I know (whether that be on *Instagram* and *TikTok*, or from the *Fictionary, Author Life*, *Rebel Author*, and *Dialogue Doctor* communities), I can't thank you enough. I won't name individuals (because I will miss someone out and feel bad about it), but you are my people, and this author's journey is much easier because of you.

Last, but never least, thank you to **YOU**, the reader, for picking up this book! I'm beyond grateful you took the time to read it, and couldn't do this without you.

About the Author

Shane Millar is an author, podcaster, writing coach, and developmental editor. He is also the author of the upcoming Grimmvale dark fantasy fairytale retellings series (writing as S. W. Millar).

Shane holds a BA in journalism and is a member of The Alliance of Independent Authors (ALLi). He lives in Buckinghamshire, England.

He has taken too many writing courses to count and enjoys reading as much as possible. As well as the writing craft, Shane is obsessed with five things: music, mythology, personal development, food, and martial arts movies.

Connect with Shane on Instagram

https://www.instagram.com/shanemillarwrites

Connect with Shane on TikTok

https://www.tiktok.com/@shanemillarwrites

Visit Shane's Website

https://writebetterfiction.com

References

Books

Alexander, J. (2018). *Self-Published Millionaire*. Self-published.

Best, M. S. (2022). *Stop Making Others Rich*. Better Best Press.

Black, S. (2020). *The Anatomy of Prose*. Atlas Black Publishing.

Cameron-Kitchen, T. and Ivanescu, Y. (2015). *Profitable Social Media Marketing*. Exposure Publishing.

Cohen, B. (2016). *How to Write a Sizzling Synopsis*. Best Page Forward LLC.

Cohen, B. (2022). *Self-Publishing with Amazon Ads.* Best Page Forward LLC.

Croft, A. (2018). *Her Last Tomorrow.* Self-published.

Gabrielle, G. (2017). *Kindle Bestseller Publishing*. Happy Dolphin Enterprises LLC.

Gaughran, D. (2019). *BookBub Ads Expert*. Self-published.

Gaughran, D. (2020). *Following*. Self-published.

Hawker, L. (2014). *Gotta Read It!* Running Rabbit Press.

Magnarella, B. (2016). *Demon Moon.* Self-Published.

Margot, J. (2021). *Amazon Ads for Indie Authors*. Book Geeks Marketing.

Meeks, B. (2019). *Mastering Amazon Descriptions*. Self-Published.

Millar, S. (2022). *How to Edit Your Novel*. Tagline Publishing.

Millar, S. (2022). *How to Plot Your Novel*. Tagline Publishing.

Millar, S. (2022). *How to Write Brilliant Beginnings*. Tagline Publishing.

Millar, S. (2022). *How to Write Novels Fast*. Tagline Publishing

Millar, S. W. (2022). *The Coven's Executioner*. Tagline Publishing.

Millar, S. W. (2022). *The Demon's Shadow*. Tagline Publishing.

Millar, S. W. (2022). *The Witch's Revenge*. Tagline Publishing.

Murphy, D. (2014). *Book Cover Design Secrets You Can Use to Sell More Books.* Creativindie.

Penn, J. (2015). *Successful Self-Publishing.* Curl Up Press.Penn, J. (2017). *How to Market a Book.* Curl Up Press.

Penn, J. (2022). *How to Write a Novel.* Curl Up Press.

Platt, S., Truant J. B. and Wright, D. (2014). *Write. Publish. Repeat.* Sterling & Stone.

Rindfleisch, J. P. and Cohen, A. B. (2022). *Dark Pawn*. 9th Publishing & Associates.

Thorn, J. (2019). *How to Self-Publish.* Thorn Publishing.

Thorn, J. and Bohannon, Z. (2020). *Three Story Method*. Thorn Publishing.

Willcocks, D. (2021). *The Self-Publishing Blueprint.* Great Writers Share.

Also By Shane Millar

Write Better Fiction

The Write Better Fiction Key Beats #0.5

How to Write Brilliant Beginnings #1

How to Plot Your Novel #2

How to Write Novels Fast #3

How to Edit Your Novel #4

How to Publish Your Book #5

More *Write Better Fiction* coming soon...

Printed in Great Britain
by Amazon

41496487R00096